free advice

WITHDRAW

DEMCO

QUANTITY SALES

Most Dell books are available at special quantity discounts when purchased in bulk by corporations, organizations, or groups. Special imprints, messages, and excerpts can be produced to meet your needs. For more information, write to: Dell Publishing, 1540 Broadway, New York, NY 10036. Attention: Director, Special Markets.

INDIVIDUAL SALES

Are there any Dell books you want but cannot find in your local stores? If so, you can order them directly from us. You can get any Dell book currently in print. For a complete up-to-date listing of our books and information on how to order, write to: Dell Readers Service, Box DR, 1540 Broadway, New York, NY 10036.

free advice

· ·

BY THE ADVICE LADIES

Amy Alkon,
Marlowe Minnick, &
Caroline Johnson

A DELL TRADE PAPERBACK

The questions in this book are based upon actual problems we have heard at our street corner Advice booth. All names and places have been changed to protect the innocent . . . and the guilty.

A DELL TRADE PAPERBACK
Published by
Dell Publishing
a division of
Bantam Doubleday Dell Publishing Group, Inc.
1540 Broadway
New York, New York 10036

Library of Congress Cataloging in Publication Data

Alkon, Amy.
Free advice / by the Advice ladies, Amy Alkon, Marlowe Minnick & Caroline Johnson.
p.   cm.
ISBN 0-440-50751-0
1. Interpersonal relations—Miscellanea.   2. Man-woman relationships—Miscellanea.   3. Dating (Social customs)—Miscellanea.   I. Minnick, Marlowe.   II. Johnson, Caroline.
III. Title.
HM132.A3547   1996
646.7′7—dc20   95-43834
                                                                    CIP

Printed in the United States of America

Published simultaneously in Canada

July 1996

10   9   8   7   6   5   4   3   2   1

FFG

ACKNOWLEDGMENTS

Like many other small businesses, The Advice Ladies is a rather lean operation. Our company assets consist of a TV tray-table (our Advice table), four flea-market chairs, and a cardboard sign. The company vehicle is a Depression-era grocery cart that we use to transport our chairs to and from our Advice corner. We have no headquarters, offices, or plant, although we do have a number of conference rooms: a few bars that don't mind us buying just one glass of wine each, occupying a table for four hours, using their electrical outlets, and consuming five bowls of goldfish crackers.

Likewise, in creating this book, we are deeply grateful for the kindness and generosity of both friends and strangers:

• Our photographers: Britt Carpenter, Wendy Andringa, Andrew Shotland, Amy Alkon, and Jean Mahaux.

• The cafes, bars, and restaurants at which we've more than worn out our welcome: The No Name Bar, The Merc Bar, the bar at the Mayflower Hotel, the Rose Cafe in Venice, California, and the coffee place on 5th Avenue at 22nd Street with the big couches.

• Our agent, John Boswell, who saw a book idea in us and helped us bring it to life.

• Our lawyer and white knight, Gil Karson, who believed in us from the start, and has kept us out of trouble ever since.

• Stephanie Gunning, Betsy Bundschuh, Leslie Schnur . . . and everybody at Dell. And, of course, Jane Rosenthal, Kate Fishman, Eric Messenger, Ben Marsh, Bill Eldred, Tom Foley, Marcello Maiorani, Martin Lewis, Bran, Grant Watt from VST Power Systems, and Joe from the Broome Street Bar.

We dedicate this book to everyone who has ever fired us. Thank you!

contents

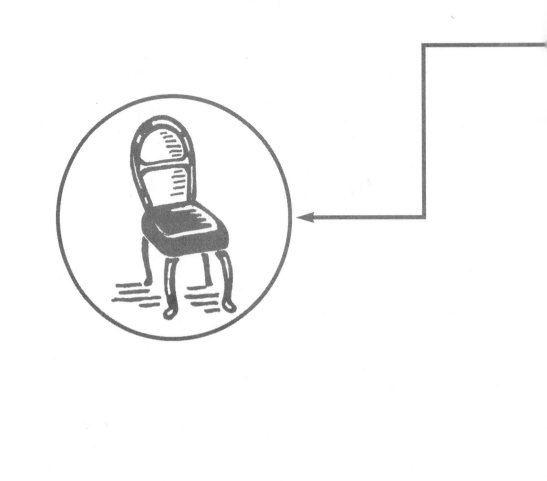

Who Are The Advice Ladies and Why Should I Take Advice from Them, Even If It Is Free?

it was one of those hot, horrible, end-of-summer nights in New York. No matter how hard we tried, nightlife kept evading us. The rest of the world was at some big party that we weren't invited to.

The three of us had become friends a few years earlier while we were all working at a large New York advertising agency. We were the company weirdoes . . . marching to the beat of our own bongos. Along with the otherworldly forces that pulled each of us to seek out new and unusual experiences, we shared a penchant for risk-taking, and a willingness to make mistakes; even to fail. We became fast friends. Together we threw off society's iron yoke of propriety, exchanged it for yards of black leather and spandex, dark glasses and fabulous earrings, and ran around looking for trouble.

Experiencing an unusually uneventful evening one rainy Friday night in downtown Manhattan, we descended upon the Moondance Diner. The place was empty, except for one depressed waiter slumped across the counter. He took our order, barely able to raise the energy to lift a requested fork. "Enjoy," he moaned.

Never ones to mind our own business, we asked him what was wrong. He sighed and began a long, sad tale of lost love. His boyfriend of several years had just dumped him. Three pairs of understanding, thickly mascara'd eyes blinked up at him with compassion. We invited him to sit down and cry on our padded shoulders. Then we went around the table and served up odd bits of common sense, a little empathy, and musings on the meaning of life. After a lengthy philosophical pep talk, we encouraged him to sweep up the scattered shards of his self-esteem, and gave him a concrete plan of action for his future.

After about fifteen minutes of our dinner-table psychology, our waiter smiled and jumped up out of his chair, a new man—in search of another new man. He thanked us and exclaimed, "Hey—you guys are good . . . you should do this for a living."

And so it began.

After he left the table, we had a little brainstorm. The following day was a Saturday. In the tradition of Lucy, from *Peanuts,* we decided to make a sign and set up a table and folding chairs on a nearby street corner and offer advice, free of charge, to anyone who wanted it. (It's pretty tough to split a nickel three ways.)

We pulled out a few markers and made a big, colorful sign. It said, in enormous letters . . . "FREE ADVICE—from a Panel of Experts . . . Presented by The Advice Ladies," and included a list of topics from Love and Dating, Fire Prevention, Nailbiting, Proper Etiquette, Office Politics to Getting Rid of Your Jerk.

We were sure no one would sit down. But at the very least, we thought we might meet a few interesting people. We chose SoHo, a Saturday-afternoon promenade district, and gravitated to the corner of West Broadway and Broome, to the sidewalk in front of an old pepper factory that stood vacant on the weekends.

To our surprise, moments after we set up, people sat down in "the advice chair"—one troubled soul after the next. On our first weekend, we managed to attract every peculiar person in SoHo. But we also spoke to quite a few "regular people" with problems. Of course, we couldn't turn

PHOTO: AMY ALKON

THE ADVICE LADIES PRESENT
FREE ADVICE
FROM A PANEL OF EXPERTS
- LOVE & DATING
- (ALSO MARRIAGE)
- GETTING RID OF YOUR JERK
- HAIR & MAKEOVERS
- PROPER ETIQUETTE
- WARDROBE CONSULTATION
- WIGS & BEARDS
- ENTERTAINING
- NEW IDENTITIES
- CONFLICT MANAGEMENT
- CAREERS
- RELOCATING
- FIRE PREVENTION
- FINANCIAL EMBARRASSMENT
- APARTMENT ENVY
- OFFICE POLITICS
- PRACTICAL JOKES
- ADVERTISING CAMPAIGNS
- BABY NAMES
- NEW PURCHASE CRITIQUES
- RISK TAKING
- EXCESSIVE HAIR
- INVOLUNTARY HAIR LOSS
- DOG COUTURE
- NEGATIVITY LESSONS: (LEARNING TO SAY NO)

them away without trying to help them solve their predicaments. Our advertising backgrounds in strategic thinking and creative problem solving gave us solid tools to quickly whittle problems down and come up with strangely practical solutions. And years of earning salaries based in large part upon creating and reworking clients' images and making people and products look their best gave us a strong foundation from which to resolve important "superficial" issues—such as "Should I dye my hair red?" and "What dog fashions do you recommend?"

Also, because of our eagerness to continually "tiptoe along the edge" in the name of personal growth, among the three of us, you could say we'd made the mistakes of at least ten people. We'd humiliated ourselves on several continents. We knew every one of the really rotten guys in downtown Manhattan (as well as a hearty supply in various other cities). We'd lived numerous lifetimes of heartache and heartbreak, with the compulsive amassing of new eye shadow that comes in between. Collectively, we'd been through the ringer.

Between sneezes (shifting winds sent the pepper flakes flying), we snapped into action, mending broken hearts, recommending "wigs and beards," and suggesting electrolysis and "new identities"—while entertaining the crowd. Not only was "Advice" tremendous fun; we actually *helped people*!

We did have our doubters. Some passersby suspected we were promoting some strange new religion. Despite our insistence that we didn't even take donations, some tourists refused to believe our advice was free. One lady sneered, "Yeah, the first question's free—then they clear out your checking account on the second one."

Even the fortune-tellers from down the block came by and kicked our sign. "You're ruining our business," they screeched at us.

Friends from the ad agency would pass us and do a double take. . . . "You!!?" they'd exclaim, "—the craziest women we know—are telling *other people* what to do?!!" And finally, in disbelief, almost everyone would ask, "Why are you doing this?"

Marlowe says it best. "When I moved to New York, a friend told me, nobody on the street will look you in the eye unless they want to rob you or have sex with you." (Or perhaps both.) We told people that we wanted to change New York's image. And, to be quite frank, we were having a *great* time. A crowd of total strangers would stand and listen to us for hours. They'd laugh, clap, and cheer. None of us had experienced that level of affirmation since the first-grade class play.

The three of us also share an intense curiosity about what makes other people tick, manifested in lifetimes of eavesdropping and people-watching. At our Advice street corner, we were astonished that people were willing, even eager, to reveal themselves to us directly—and at audible levels. Men, women, and children sat down and spoke openly about their most intimate dilemmas—from love problems and sexual traumas to dealing with the curse of a hairy back. We listened and we helped them.

Soon we became fixtures in SoHo—the cottage industry for the depressed. People with problems knew where to find us: "Saturdays, in nice weather, two-thirty to five P.M., West Broadway and Broome." We established a clientele; we even had "regulars" who came to us on an ongoing basis to update us on how our advice was working. And as we go about our day-to-day business in Manhattan, it's not uncommon for us to hear a voice in the crowd yell, "Hey, Advice Lady! . . . Remember me? . . . *I did it!*"

WHAT'S YOUR PROBLEM?

Everybody's ashamed of their problems. They try to sweep them under the rug, shove them in the closet. They dream of sneaking out at midnight to bury them in the backyard.

Instead of being embarrassed about your problems, we suggest you *embrace* them. Spend some quality time together. Walk arm in arm down the street with your problem. Tickle it under the chin and purr, "Oh, what you do to me!"

To begin the process, examine your life on both deep and superficial levels. Ask yourself what areas are not perfect. There you will find your problems.

Don't be stingy with your troubles. Surely you have more than enough to go around. Share a problem with your friends. Even strangers. Introduce it at parties (maybe someone will pick it up).

Once your problem realizes it can't scare you anymore, it'll probably dump you straightaway for someone else.

What? So you think your problem is faithful to you? Your problem is probably in bed with your best friend at this very moment! And it's jetting

PHOTO: BRITT CARPENTER

No hole is deep enough to bury a problem once and for all.

off to the south of France next week with the girl next door. Problems are fickle little fellows.

When you get rid of the dilemmas now plaguing you, actively seek out new ones to replace them. When you're problem-free—*that's* a problem. To us, it means that you're not living hard enough.

This book is your guide to creatively get down and dirty with, then give the boot to, your minor and more monumental woes. But the advice here isn't meant to be taken as if engraved in stone brought down from on high. We came by it through going out, taking risks, occasionally even making fools of ourselves, then scrutinizing the process in hindsight. We hope you'll make our answers work for you in your own lives, maybe even improve upon them, by doing the same.

Just one more preliminary word of advice. Don't take yourself too seriously. We think solving your problems should be fun. If all else fails, you can always start your own church.

Here's to your troubles. **— THE ADVICE LADIES**

HOW TO USE THIS BOOK

Turn the page. Start reading. As soon as you see advice that works for you, put it into practice.

Instead of following the standard book format, we've chosen to give our Advice in whatever format worked best for the topic in question—be it a list, a letter, a chart, a photograph, or a funny story about something that happened to one of us.

By the way, one of our credos is "Go ahead and humiliate yourself." You'll live. We're sure that dying of embarrassment is one of the lowest death statistics on record. We're living proof. Our own humiliations run the gamut from horrible to hilarious, as you'll see in the stories we've included about ourselves. When these stories are first person, we've indicated which one of us is telling the tale.

Now, pour your problem a beer and curl up on the couch together with this book. Hopefully, halfway through the book, you may even find yourself all alone.

BEST OF LUCK!

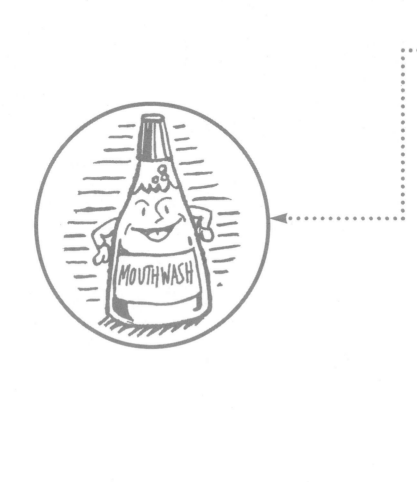

CHAPTER 1

Getting Yourself Ready to Interact with Others

One sunny SoHo Saturday, a young guy in his early twenties slumped into our Advice chair, gloomier than a lost dog. He pulled out a creased photo and asked, "Have you seen this woman?" Head hanging, he mumbled his problem into the pavement. He'd had a fight with his girlfriend. He told us that he'd gone back to her apartment to apologize for some things he'd said, but she wasn't home, so he wrote her a short note of apology.

"Great!" the three of us said in unison.

"What did it say?" one of us sympathetically inquired.

Frowning, Mr. Gloom hung his heavy head even lower and muttered, " 'Hate me, I suck.' "

A lot of people sit down in our chair and talk about their love problems:

- How do you know if you're really in love?
- Where should I go to meet people?
- How do you keep a long-term relationship fresh?
- I'm in love with two women. Why can't I have both?

However, before you go hunting for the answers to the big questions about your relationships with others, you need to start with you. Ironically, the thing that makes people run from our chair faster than anything else is the suggestion "Now let's focus on *you*."

Who are you? Are you really ready to reveal yourself to the outside world? Liking you has got to start at home. Would you be pleased to make your acquaintance? If you proposed to yourself, what would your answer be?

A lot of people assume that entering into a relationship with another person will be the solution to all of their problems—loneliness, depression, something that's missing in their lives—but only when you fill your own internal void will you be fit company for someone else.

So, before you run off to meet the rest of the world, spend some time alone getting to know *you*. Talk to yourself. (Preferably not in public.) Your goal should be to get to a point at which you're not lonely anymore when you're all by yourself. Ask yourself a lot of questions—as if you're a stranger whom you've just met.

Ten questions to ask yourself to get to know yourself better

1. What are the ten most essential things you know about life?

2. What wouldn't you want anyone to know about you?

3. What's missing from your life?

4. What do you like most about yourself? Dislike most?

5. What would you trade your life for, and why?

6. What qualities are most important to you in another person?

7. If you could invite any five women, alive or dead, to dinner, who would they be? Any five men?

8. What would you title the movie based on your life?

9. If you could accomplish only one thing in your lifetime, what would it be?

10. If you had an hour left to live, what would you do in that hour?

"HELLO," FELLOW HUMANS

On an average day, if you could read the thought bubble over everyone's head, you'd probably find the likes of . . .

"They're all thinking these glasses make me look like an insect."
"Everyone on this bus knows I haven't had sex for two years."
"They can all see my underwear through these pants!"

Once you realize that everyone is too busy focusing on their own shortcomings to dwell upon yours, you will understand that the blemish on your chin is not likely to make the front page of the *National Enquirer.*

Suppose somebody catches your eye in a café. If you lean over and say hello, what's the worst thing that could happen? That person isn't likely to turn around, laugh uproariously at you, and call to the other patrons, "Hey, everybody, did you hear what that buffoon in the dueling plaids just said to me!?"

Don't put off meeting people until you feel really bored and lonely. New, interesting people will not materialize, genie style, the moment you're finally ready to meet them. Take action now!

Think about all of the times that you've yearned after some attractive stranger walking away from you, and out of your life forever. If only you could turn back the clock, gather up some guts, open your lips, and utter that oh-so-monumental word:

"Hello"

It's not half as overwhelming as it sounds.

"CALLING OUT THE STOPS"

by MARLOWE

Under deep hypnosis, I'm almost certain my shyness can be traced back to eleven p.m. Eastern standard time, December 30, 1958. I was embarrassed to be born. My entire life has been a string of embarrassing moments linked together with thoughts of unzipping my skin and running out screaming.

Upon moving to New York, I discovered that the famous shrink and author of all the self-help books I'd read growing up was available for private consultations. I lunged at the opportunity, hoping for a cure.

My seventy-something Buddha explained to me that nobody really cares what you do; they're all obsessed with themselves.

He gave me two exercises to do before our next session. First, I was to get on the subway and call out all the stops. My other task was to walk up to a complete stranger on the street and say, "I just got out of the mental hospital . . . do you know what month it is?" When I challenged the absurdity of these tests, he asked, "Would you do it for a million dollars?"

"Of course I would," I replied.

"Just do it," he answered, as he pried me from the couch and escorted me out of the office.

Almost a week had gone by. I had put off humiliating myself as long as possible. I was headed home on the subway after having a few cocktails. This was it. My big chance.

I shifted nervously as the train approached the Fiftieth Street station. Just as I was about to speak, an alien from outer space, in purple tights, a green vest, and Ping-Pong ball antennae leapt inside playing an excoriating version of "My Favorite Things" on the saxophone. Instead of seizing this distraction as an opportunity, I used it as the perfect excuse to delay my announcement one more stop. I rehearsed silently as the "alien" forced donations by continuing to play.

A crowd of passengers pushed toward the door, to get out at

Forty-second Street. As they made their chaotic exit, I called out, "Forty-second Street . . . Times Square."

The doors banged shut. Silence followed. The remaining passengers in the now sparsely populated car turned in my direction, unsure of whether the sound had come from me or from the man who had just entered the car selling glow-in-the-dark spinning-tops for a dollar. I regained my composure, and also cast a suspicious glance at him.

At the next stop, no longer a novice, I called out "Thirty-fourth Street" a little louder. Next I shouted, "Twenty-eighth Street." By this time, any passengers still left probably thought I was truly insane as I sat crossing and uncrossing my arms and legs all over the place, alternating episodes of neurotic giggling in between failed attempts at a poker-faced deadpan.

I ran out of the car at Fourteenth Street. I felt like a total lunatic. I felt wonderful.

By noon the next day, my newfound self-confidence had already worn off. I was walking to my appointment, desperately searching Madison Avenue for a stranger to ask what month it was. Bypassing chic shops and women in mandatory Chanel, I spotted my unwitting target.

Steadying myself, I approached the small, hunched prehistoric gentleman in the polka-dotted clown suit, handing out flyers. As he held the fluttering paper to my face with his trembling hands, I was rendered speechless and fled up the street. *Intimidated by a clown,* I thought. *This is truly pathetic.* Plus a clown didn't really count anyway.

I saw my man a block and a half away. He was different from the rest; tall, but curiously limp at the neck; his clothing a set of checkerboards, paisleys, and polka dots, duking it out on his chest. Behind thick, greasy black glasses, he seemed bewildered. What if he *doesn't* know what month it is? I thought to myself.

"Excuse me," I mumbled, focusing on the pavement.

"I just got out of the mental hospital . . . do you know what month it is?"

> Under deep hypnosis, I'm almost certain my shyness can be traced back to eleven p.m. Eastern standard time, December 30, 1958. I was embarrassed to be born.

I glanced up at him from the cement, but without enough composure to look him directly in the eye.

"What month is it?" he questioned, staring down at me intently.
"It's Awwwwgust!"

Relieved, I smiled and bounced up Madison Avenue.

"It's August, it's August!" What a feeling of freedom I had. The
Brooklyn Bridge didn't fall down, buildings didn't explode, manhole
covers didn't blow off . . . everything was exactly the same.

If you consider yourself shy, it helps to keep in mind that *everybody* is
insecure. The same person you're terrified to approach is very likely
equally petrified to talk to you. Look back at somebody you've met, who,
from a distance, looked to you to be Cary Grant's next of kin . . . probably
on a Rhodes scholarship. As you got to know this person better and better, he transformed into the "Incredible Shrinking Man," growing smaller
and smaller in your eyes . . . until he nearly vanished.

The next time you long to meet some intriguing stranger, fuel your
courage to introduce yourself with all of your memories of other apparent
towers of wit, intellect, and good looks who shriveled in magnitude as
soon as you made their acquaintance. If you're especially timid, try a little
remedial work to get into the swing of things. . . .

OUR SUGGESTED HOMEWORK FOR SHY PEOPLE

Quit taking refuge in prekindergarten warnings from your parents against
talking to strangers. That stuff only applies before you hit puberty—
which, these days, apparently happens at around eight years of age.

Every day, force yourself to speak to three new people. If you're
terribly shy, start with those who are almost guaranteed not to
spurn anyone's attention; the homebound . . . the institutionalized
. . . neighborhood dogs . . . and work your way up from there. Af-

ter a few weeks of diligent practice, you'll be a pro, or at least you'll see from experience that it's not so earth-shattering to try to make someone's acquaintance and start a little friendly conversation. Once you've experimented on a few easy guinea pigs, move on to people who actually interest you.

Make it easy for your target to comfortably continue the conversation beyond your greeting. Thus, try *not* to ask questions that can be answered with a simple yes or no. For example . . .

"Are you Fred?"

Ninety-four point three percent of all Americans you'll ask are not. Your chances get even bleaker on a global scale. Most people will shoot you down with a quick no and move on.

BORING BUT USEFUL CONVERSATIONAL CRUTCHES
(To Hold You Up Until Your IQ Gets Back from the Liquor Store)

If your brains and wit ditch you the moment you spot someone you like, stall your quarry with one of the following easy emergency options. If you're lucky, her response may provoke the return of your consciousness.

- Flattery. Compliment the person on something—anything—whether or not you find it attractive. "I love your _____." (For example: chartreuse and lilac houndstooth tie, bestiality bowling shirt, pet armadillo.)
- Ask him if he's tried an exotic new product in the store. (You may not want to hear the answer if you're shopping in a medical supply house.)
- Ask her if you know her face—from television.
- Ask him where he purchased some item he's wearing.
- Ask her directions.
- Ask him anything, but ask him something!

IS YOUR AURA A LITTLE TOO INSTITUTIONAL GREEN?

To improve your success rate, make sure the persona you project is warm and friendly. If your expression says, *Every day is a funeral for me,* people will ransack their pockets for garlic and crosses when they see you coming.

"THE FILM STRIP"

by AMY

I had finally given an on-again/off-again boyfriend the ejection seat. Marlowe, Caroline, and I were invited to a downtown French film-screening and cocktail reception. Feeling a little lonely, I fantasized that I might meet some thrilling *nouveau homme* at the reception, who would spirit me off through foggy Parisian streets for a night of mystery and romance.

I dressed for the evening with visions of The Paris Collections in mind—assembling my outfit from various filmy items I had purchased at the ten-dollar store and accessorizing it with several pieces of recycled kitchenware.

I pranced off in my $26.98 finery to join Marlowe and Caroline for margaritas. With mock haughtiness, I paraded into the restaurant, twirling my gauzy fashion adventure down the imaginary catwalk leading to Marlowe and Caroline's table, sniffing disdainfully at the hungry hoards of international fashion reporters that only I could see.

"Stunning," Marlowe greeted me.

"Très belle," affirmed Caroline.

"It's not see-through?" I asked.

"Oh, no," Caroline reassured me.

Upon finishing our drinks, we left the restaurant to walk to the screening. Outside, in the bright light of day, Caroline hooted. "Amy . . . I hate to tell you this, but you can see absolutely everything!" Marlowe and Caroline howled with laughter.

Banished from my fashion Eden, I sulked all the way to the screening, attempting with one hand to cover my peekaboo butt with my backpack while I tried to nonchalantly camouflage full frontal nudity with the other.

"It's not see-through?" I asked.

At the cocktail party, I took refuge in a dark corner, pretending to be transfixed by a tattered copy of *The New York Times,* which I held open in front of me. Peering over the faded pages, I tried to console myself with the thought that Jill Goodacre, another lingerie model, had ended up with Harry Connick, Jr.

Scowling, I eyed the crowd. The whole room appeared to be filled with happy couples playfully popping hors d'oeuvres into each other's mouths. Suddenly, from across the room, a nearsighted guy, in a greenish leisure suit of extremely unnatural origin, eagle-eyed me in the corner. *Maybe he's got a thing for strippers,* I surmised.

With dogged determination, he tackled the thick crowd between us. I grimaced, then I caught myself. He might be a nice guy, I thought, beating down a sizable wave of self-pity. Maybe he just needs a makeover.

I watched him shove his way through the masses, my stomach churning with alternating twinges of gratitude and dread. Hey, be open, I lectured myself. Strike up a conversation. You never know.

Glassy eyed, he strode the final paces toward me. I nervously smoothed my paper-fronted peignoir.

"Hey . . ." he said.

I peered at him over my Metro-section wall. "Hi!" I stuttered, summoning superhuman effort to lift the corners of my mouth into a feeble imitation of a smile.

". . . Got the movie section there?" he continued.

"Just the local section," I responded, punctuating my words with fluttering eyelashes. "Are you—"

"Oh, well!" he interrupted. "Thanks anyway." He whirled around and disappeared as quickly as he'd come. Finding myself, once again, a seminude lone wolf, I slunk back into my paneled cave to marinate in my humiliation.

WIPING THE EGG OFF YOUR FACE

While the three of us can tell you that it's certainly a lot easier to tell other people to laugh at their embarrassments than it is to take that advice oneself, your sense of humor is usually your best defense when your miniskirt flies up and reveals your red polka-dotted thong underwear to the lunching construction crew. Moreover, if you're the one who *starts* laughing at your problem, others can only join in. That's the best way to ensure that they're laughing *with* you—not just at you.

THE CONVERSATION

To meet interesting people *you* have to be interesting. If you lead a full life, you'll always have something to say. However, if you plant yourself in front of a TV set every night, your conversation is likely to resemble a string of tag lines from commercials.

ARE YOU BORING?

If your life seems dull and empty, evict yourself from your living room. Make an effort to seek out adventure. This, however, doesn't mean you should start a bar brawl. While a black eye and a couple of broken ribs may be a new experience for you, that experience is unlikely to expand anything beyond your doctor's wallet.

You'll find adventure by testing your physical and emotional boundaries. What are you afraid of? What makes you really uncomfortable? Don't let your fears and limitations fence you in. Whatever activities or things are a little beyond your reach, those are the things you should strive to experience. And as soon as you attain a goal, or get beyond one of your fears, mark a new and slightly more terrifying height to scale. Challenging your limits is a lifelong job—if you're one of those people who are convinced that there's more to being alive than simply continuing to breathe.

Parachute, pose nude, say "I love you." Take classes—either ones that passionately interest you or, better yet, ones that seem totally outside of your range. For example, if you're shy and retiring, you might try a stand-up comedy class. If you're an excitable, overly gregarious type, challenge your nature in a meditation workshop. If you've got a bunch of guy friends best known for their ability to order carryout Chinese, drag them off to cooking school. To expand your horizons, try going by the following rule: If the shoe fits, toss it aside and look for a new one that will take some growing into.

Don't assume that you have to leave the house to find new mountains to climb. For at-home adventuring, remove some of those books you've been using to prop up your TV and take a look between the covers. If you feed your mind, it will be more likely to come to your assistance when your ego needs it most.

The next time you automatically reach for the remote control, instead sit yourself down in a big chair and dream. Write your own fantasies. Think up some mischief. Drag all of your old skeletons out of your closet and give them notice that they're about to be replaced.

After reawakening your sleeping brain cells by experiencing adventures and thinking original thoughts, you're likely to tire of watching imaginary people live their fictional half-hour lives on a two-by-two plastic box. At that point, you may long to acquaint yourself with the lost art of conversation.

How To Converse

Before the advent of the Internet, on which acronyms like ROFLOL (Rolling on Floor Laughing Out Loud) are used to indicate that one finds a remark rather humorous, conversation used to be considered a face-to-face verbal exchange between two or more people. One person would inquire about the other person's life, interests, and beliefs, and actually *listen* to the other person's replies, then respond in turn.

These days, whether on-line or in person, many people confuse conversation with simply talking, or even worse, lecturing. Such people are also usually the ones who interrupt others at whim. It is bad form to interrupt someone else's speech without very good reason. Good reason can be defined as something like the following: If, while engaged in conversation, you notice someone stealing your car, you may want to break in with "Excuse me, I'll be right back," in lieu of dashing off in a dead run without explanation.

When you meet someone who interests you, it's a good idea to ply that person with interesting conversation to increase the likelihood that he or she will return your interest—or at very least, stay awake while you're talking. Here are a few of our suggestions:

I N T E R E S T I N G   C O N V E R S A T I O N

- Each other (P.S. If this is not interesting, find someone else to talk to)
- Books not sold at supermarket checkouts
- Philosophers not seen on TV
- Things you'd like to invent
- Where to find the best martini
- Weird things you've seen on the street
- What you'd eat at your Last Supper
- Kitsch motels (like the Space Age Lodge in Anaheim, next to Disneyland—and its lonely twin in Gila Bend, Arizona)
- Worst job you've ever held
- Fantasy jobs you wouldn't dare write home about
- What creatures the people in the room resemble
- Most recent embarrassment

THINGS NOT TO TALK ABOUT

- Astrological compatibility

- Meeting yearly sales quotas

- Da Mets

- Der Führer

- Celebrity gossip on a first-name basis

- Any recent surgery

- The great sex you had with your ex

- Why the other person should quit smoking or drinking

- Percentage of fat in McDonald's hamburgers

- Last arrest or incarceration

- Why you can't get over your last relationship

- Your ex-wife's childbirth

- Dental humor

"HELMUT"

Most people manage to commit only one conversational faux pas at a time. However, the three of us had drinks with a man in L.A. who managed to break each and every "rule" in the course of one long and torturous cocktail hour.

Helmut was six four, tanned and fortyish, with long blond curly hair that he wore in a ponytail. Amy met him while skating on the beach. In the glow of the setting sun over the Pacific, he looked like Thor.

He showed up at our hotel wearing what appeared to be his holy communion suit. His jacket was too tight and his pants were too short, revealing thick, police-car-blue acrylic socks and brown plastic shoes with tiny gold insignia stapled to them—the kind usually found tied together in a bin.

The three of us each ordered a glass of wine. In a thick German accent Helmut proudly demanded a seltzer. As soon as the waitress left with our order, he self-righteously railed against the health hazards of alcohol consumption. He warned us that alcohol had been proved to cause premature wrinkling and birth defects. Each of us surreptitiously checked our skin for early warning signs from our breakfast Mimosa.

Helmut told us that he was an expert on health and fitness, and dropped names of all the famous people he had trained. Then, without the least bit of prompting, he immediately launched into a diatribe on the evil ways Americans bring up their children. He pounded his chest with pride, regaling us with glorious tales of how *he* had raised his two children, because he knew he could do a better job than his wife. Before we could jump in to change the rather offensive subject, it got worse. He described in detail how he had assisted in—or rather, orchestrated—his wife's childbirth. "I vas there. I vashed da blood off da fetus!"

Helmut left no bodily function unmentioned. Without a pause, he leapt into a lengthy reproductive-issues lecture—beginning with AIDs and continuing on to contraceptive methodology. "Condoms, condoms, condoms!" he cried in a volume that sent vibrations through our wineglasses. "Dat's all ve hear!"

He informed us that we are all brainwashed by the U.S. government into using condoms and expensive, complicated devices for birth control. He claimed that, for birth control purposes, what "we" really need is for all women to use basal thermometers (describing the process in rather graphic detail)—again proudly reinforcing his closeness with the human body.

We had a brief moment of physiological relief when he dipped into the topic of taxes, but somehow he managed to turn his opinions on the ills of the American monetary system into yet another lecture on the cervical opening.

Then he plunged headfirst once again into the remaining evils of America—blaming all societal ills on Toyota and McDonald's, whom he suspected were engaged in a corporate conspiracy to take over the world. "Oh . . . vat a fee-ling!" he sneered. He intimated that the success of McDonald's was a government plot; that Ronald McDonald was an evil clown, distributing poison to the masses in the form of "happy meals."

Caroline was the only one who still had the strength to fight back. "I like McDonald's!" she bellowed.

As he took a deep breath before launching into his next lecture, we finally managed to grab the floor just long enough to politely extricate ourselves from his conversational claws. We stood up, informing him that the three of us had to depart, as we'd been invited to attend a close friend's party. Suddenly, his pedantic demeanor took an unexpectedly congenial turn. He bounced up from the couch. "Vere are ve goingk?" he asked cheerfully.

> He showed up at our hotel wearing what appeared to be his holy communion suit. His jacket was too tight and his pants were too short, revealing thick, police-car-blue acrylic socks and brown plastic shoes with tiny gold insignia stapled to them—the kind usually found tied together in a bin.

Astonished, we muttered polite "invitation only" apologies and left Helmut with only his beloved glass of seltzer for company.

BAD LINES

Some people feel incapable of introducing themselves to another person without employing a witty, Nobel-prize-winning opening line (nominated for humor that stretches the laws of physics). While humor is almost always a good thing, such opening lines tend to come across as a bit stilted, and may give the recipient the idea that the purveyor has been up all night cribbing bits from old Noel Coward plays.

The following are some memorable (and mostly unsuccessful) opening lines we have heard over the years. Just remember, the point is to connect with another human being, not to rival Henny Youngman.

- Pardon me, but are you wearing thong underwear?

- If I were a mosquito I would bite you.

  (Response: If you were a mosquito, I would swat you.)

- Never seen a body like that on a white woman.

- Can I talk to you about your figure for a moment?

- How 'bout some fries with that shake?

- Can I count your freckles?

- Excuse me, but are you my ex-wife?

- You seem like the kind of girl who likes to eat cold pizza for breakfast.

- I'd like to wrap your thighs around my face.

- What time should I set the alarm for?

- Me Tarzan, you Jane. How about it?

- Big white woman!

- You remind me of a panther raised in captivity.

- Are we going to have connubial relations?

  (Us: Why, yes . . . just as soon as we stop laughing.)

CLOSING THE SALE

If you hit it off with someone you meet, be sure to ask her for her number *and* offer her yours so you can arrange to reconnoiter to get to know each other even better.

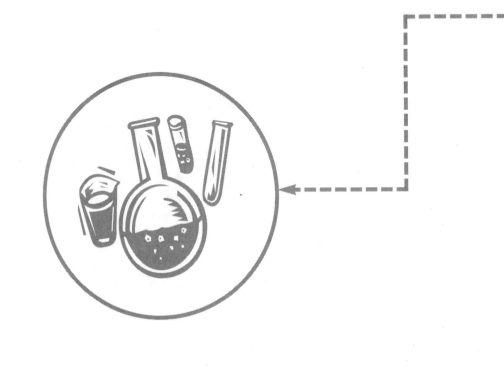

CHAPTER 2

--- Reinventing You

POSITIONING THE SELF IN THE MARKETPLACE

Our collective advertising background has given us some insight into the minds of consumers. By following the same guidelines set forth in selling, say, an ordinary can of baked beans, you can change the way you are perceived by the marketplace.

Often it's not what's in the can that differentiates one product from another, but rather the image a product projects. A sexy name, a bright, colorful label, or even a phallic package can create an aura of desirability, contrasted with the typical dull Brand-X product.

The humble sixty-nine-cent can of baked beans arrives at the advertising agency on the verge of extinction. It gets dusted off, polished up, and emerges magically transformed as the heroic legume—the latest trend in "casual entertaining." This is achieved by what ad agencies call "repositioning."

Let us illustrate this process by using an extreme example—a man we will call "Herman." Let's pretend Herman is in dire need of repositioning;

in fact, you could say he shares some of the characteristics of the lowly baked bean (including being cheap and having an unpleasant aftereffect).

The first thing to define is the current consumer perception
(how you come across to others).

Herman is a dull, unattractive, sullen, overweight, insufferable, cheap, pretentious boor—with whom I have no desire to associate.

Now let's contrast that with the desired consumer perception
(what do you *want* people to think about you?).

Herman is a handsome, svelte, gregarious, sensitive (but not too), generous "life of the party" with whom I desire to spend time whenever possible.

OUR MISSION

Change "consumer" perception of Herman and convince people that by associating with Herman and basking in his virtues, they will improve the quality of their lives.

TARGET AUDIENCE

Before venturing forth, determine who is most likely to be in the market for a Herman. Assuming that the entire world is not your desired consumer, hone your perspective to include only the most likely and desirable candidates.

In Herman's case, his target is limited to a most exclusive group: all women of childbearing years.

Also remember that you must seek out places where you will come in contact with your target. It could be that you are perfectly fetching, but simply have a visibility problem. This is not a problem for Herman—due to the largeness of his posterior, he is more than visible in a crowd.

GET TO KNOW YOUR PRODUCT

To develop your strategy, you must take a careful inventory of the product's points of appeal. Make a list illuminating the product's virtues while downplaying its shortcomings. For example, we know that Herman plays the tuba. In order to catalog this in the virtue column, we will henceforth refer to this ability as "having a musical sensitivity expressed in the brass section."

Herman also has a complete collection of every plastic NFL beer mug ever available in a "thirsty two-ouncer." This virtue will now be referred to as: "a limited collection of carbon-based beer steins embossed with the noble crest of modern-day warriors."

Another interesting fact about Herman is that he also owns a goldfish that he won with a Ping-Pong ball at the county fair, and a small turtle from Woolworth's that he was pet-sitting, which the owner never reclaimed. We will refer to these with "Herman has an extraordinary collection of fauna, both amphibious and aquatic creatures, that he studies to measure the effect of habitat changes on behavior."

PHOTOS: WENDY ANDRINGA

FIGURE A. BEFORE Habitat modification   **FIGURE B. AFTER Habitat modification**

Unique Point of Difference

In advertising, we look for what is called a unique point of difference—*the one thing* you want consumers to remember about the product. Pick one thing, and only one. In Herman's case, it could be the tuba, or his zoological pursuits, or other esoteric hobbies. Or it could be that Herman is always seen in an interesting hat, unusually patterned shoes, or a different pair of eyeglasses every day. Dressing in monochromatic colors is another way to stand out. A red jumpsuit, red hat and shoes one day—and a blueberry ensemble the next. At present, Herman is known for the abstract catsup stains that adorn his faded vintage clothing. Instead, when Herman strolls down the boulevard, we would rather people remark, "There goes Herman. Did you know that he has an amazing collection of antique Mormon underwear?"

Packaging

In the eighties, when America was really workout crazy, many corporations "beefed up" their product mascots so consumers could better identify with them. Scrawny cartoon animals selling cereal suddenly sported impressive biceps to compete with the virile image of a competitor with a larger market share.

In a similar fashion, it would be advisable for Herman to take a trip or two to the gym to modify his profile into something, perhaps, less "elephantine." Whereas "12 ounces free!" may be an intriguing offer on a cereal box, "12 lbs. less" may be equally appealing when marketing Herman.

Or as a product will change its package for a totally new look, the same might be in order for Herman. This could run the gamut from a new haircut to a new wardrobe. Herman may choose to redo his "can"—in a totally mod look.

You can even go so far as changing your name. Sometimes the name you were given is simply unsuitable to describe yourself. No one wants to reach for a product called "Buttwipe"; however, it flies off the shelves as "White Cloud." That's why they named ordinary tuna "Chicken of the

Sea." A jar of "Herman" might be in great demand stylishly relabeled "Maurice." You can almost hear people saying, "Oooh . . . it sounds imported."

TONE AND MANNER

The last thing to consider in executing your strategy is "tone and manner." Do you want to shout your message boldly? Are you a giant starburst with the word *Free* in sixty-point type? Here comes Herman . . . he's 50% thinner (today only)!

Are you quiet and sophisticated, classic, or trendy and flashy? Be consistent in how you deliver your message, and you will better establish your personality in the eyes of others.

In summary, if Herman redoes his image—creates a new package, new name, new look—and positions himself in locations where he is likely to come in contact with his target audience (anywhere but a mens' club or an elementary school), he should soon find consumers seeking him out with the same zeal shoppers express at a one-day white sale. Otherwise he'll be doomed to remain another marked-down china elephant, neglected on the basement clearance table.

"THE FANTASY YOU"

A business-school friend of Caroline's sat down at our Advice table. He was tall, with a thin, rather elegant face, and sandy hair in casual retreat; a WASP-Prep, down to the turtleneck and tweed blazer. There was something about his polite, affable manner that was reminiscent of a bygone era.

A week before, he revealed, he had been fired from what he described as his "dull Wall Street job." He admitted that he was actually rather relieved, as he had been considering a career change for quite some time. He was now using his extended leisure to take a little personal inventory.

Perusing our Advice sign, he raised an eyebrow at the words *New Identities.*

He took a contemplative puff of his cigarette, and as he continued to muse about changing his life, he ripple-dissolved into William Powell before our very eyes.

Infused with inspiration, we began spinning a web of intrigue about him. Part of what makes a person interesting, we told him, is making everyone wonder, *Who is he? Where has he just been?*

You're suave, you're debonair, we said. Your milieu is martinis and witty repartee at the club . . . until dawn. You should forever be seen entering your apartment at eight A.M., and always in a tuxedo and a loosened bow tie—even if it means going out the service exit a half hour earlier to make your stunning reentry.

While others trudge alongside their pets in worn sweatpants and helmets of pink curlers, you will earn a reputation as the unsolved mystery of the neighborhood canine contingent—the only man oft seen sporting a pooper-scooper while garbed in rumpled tails.

We asked his name. Richard. We yawned collectively and suggested a few substitutions, more in keeping with the era of his

new identity . . . Tyrone . . . Alistair . . . perhaps something along the
lines of . . . "Bing."

Matter-of-factly, he told us his middle name was Errol.

"Oh, that's so fabulous!!" we agreed. "Oh . . . yes, yes, yes!"

He was taken aback for a moment. Then he sat up a little
straighter in his chair and crossed his legs, feeling the Errol within
him taking command.

Forget the banking thing, we continued. It's a bore. Now
you own the nightlife. Open up a posh supper club. We can
see it now: ERROL'S in white script on the black scalloped awning.

When the inclination strikes you, you'll come up front to greet the
beautiful dames at the door. That is, when you're not in the back
room, negotiating clandestine deals. There's always a chilled martini
waiting for you at the end of the bar. A doll with a sad story to tell.
And the band's always playing your song.

He resisted the urge to lean forward.

We continued at breakneck pace. Fortunately, he lived in the old-
money section of the Upper East Side, so he merely had to
redecorate his current apartment to fit his new personality. Go Deco,
we advised. Toss your La-Z-Boy aside for a chaise lounge. Throw
Herculon over for black velvet. Monogram everything with an
ornate, scripted *E.*

But think beyond martini glasses and the expected silver cigarette
lighter. Go for the doorknobs, the toilet seat covers, your hubcaps,
your Tupperware, and your toaster. Bribe the super to paint a huge
script *E* on your mailbox.

Think of the adventures that await you, we exclaimed. We
provided him with a list of *Thin Man* films to study for reference, as
well as a map to establishments trafficking in secondhand tuxedos.

Still a bit skeptical about the promise of his new life, Errol
thanked us, got up, and hurried off. Moments later, we couldn't help
but notice him in the distance, unable to resist the urge to light a
lady's cigarette. We're not sure whether or not he heard our
applause.

WHO SAYS YOU SHOULD "JUST BE YOURSELF?"

If you feel a little bored with the same old you, why not graduate to the next logical step and sample what it's like "being someone else"? Choose your new persona from dozens of well-honed characters available at your local video store, bookstore, or library:

SAMPLE IDENTITIES

Operativos Privados: Do the private detective thing . . . with style. Accessorize your tightly cinched Calvin Klein trench coat with miniature electronic accessories, such as walkie-talkies and listening devices, available at stores like The Sharper Image, with a thirty-day no-questions-asked money-back return policy. We like to think of it as a twenty-nine-day contemplating purchase plan.

The Urban Clint Eastwood: Go Spaghetti Western—unshaven, sunburnt, wearing weathered clothing and muddy boots. Practice squinting while gnawing on a cheroot. Accurate role recreation requires little witty conversation, as Clint never did have much to say.

Movie Star: Delve into Hollywood's golden past to create the new you. Model yourself after Harlow, Dietrich, Monroe, Veronica Lake. Clark Gable, Cary Grant . . .

> Say you chose Fred Astaire. You might sing and dance down the sidewalks with an umbrella until they lock you up for disturbing the peace. Turn mundane chores into song—sing for your sandwich at the deli, tap-dance the answer to "One lump or two?"

Get a few friends with cameras to follow you, point, and whisper. If you closely resemble any current movie idols, use their names to make restaurant reservations, and you will get highly desirable tables.

James Bond: This character requires an enormous wardrobe, as James is known to change his outfit at least once every five minutes. Start with a blue blazer with brass buttons, slicked-back hair, and a martini. Go from tuxedo to bathrobe, safari jacket to polo outfit to yacht wear. Scuba gear may be rather cumbersome in urban areas.

Movie Director: This one's simple. A Panavision baseball hat (available at motion-picture camera rental houses), sunglasses, and three-days' growth is all you need. (Hidden receding hairline will be taken for granted.) Same goes for women directors, except, hopefully, for the receding hairline and three days' growth.

Plantation Owner: A pith helmet, linen suit, wire-rim sunglasses, and a cane. If you've got a little money, rent a migrant worker to carry you home after drowning in rum and tonics at that hotel bar with the palms and ceiling fans.

Sea Captain: Of the sailboat kind. This is a good excuse for the weathered skin you got while ignoring all those warnings about too much sun. Grow an unkempt beard that looks like you trimmed it with a Swiss army knife. Go for windblown sun-bleached hair, utility sunglasses on a string, a tattered canvas duffel bag, and worn, faded once-expensive clothing. Throw a bit of sand in your hair and on your clothing.

Liberace: Glue glitter and sequins on everything you own. Take a few music lessons, then carry a candelabra to restaurants and offer to give free concerts.

Big Rig Operator: You'll need a worn T-shirt, a John Deere hat, and a big gut. Hang out at the highway ham-and-egger. Only shower at truck-stop cafés.

Paparazzo: Wear a khaki vest—the kind with dozens of ferret-sized utility pockets. String several cameras around your neck. Furtively follow complete nobodies and photograph them doing mundane chores.

Royalty: Trade off with a friend on this one. One of you is queen for a day, the other is lowly servant, package carrier, and chauffeur—in uniform, of course.

Assume a Character from a Movie: If you seek further inspiration, plumb your video store for a few new ideas.

Fay Dunaway as *Mommie Dearest*

Audrey Hepburn in *Breakfast at Tiffany's*

Jeremy Brett as *Sherlock Holmes*

Bogart, of course, in *Casablanca*

Cruella de Vil from *One Hundred and One Dalmatians*

Marlon Brando in almost any role

Crocodile Dundee

Betty Boop (before the censors got to her)

Jessica Rabbit

Uniform sale and rental houses can provide endless options and weeks of fun. Become a Rear Admiral for a day. Or an Ambulance Driver, Security Guard, or Mercenary.

"WHAT'S IN A NAME?"

by MARLOWE

Several years ago, I spent a month traveling alone in Spain. On my first night in Madrid, I explored the nightlife through the narrow, winding streets. Within a few blocks, I began to feel that a man was following me, and I ducked into one of the many colorful unmarked doors that held the promise of exotic elixirs behind them.

I found a seat at the bar and pulled out a cigarette. No sooner had the cigarette touched my lips, than the presence I had felt earlier materialized with a flaming lighter. Looking up the outstretched arm before me, I saw the smile of a Spanish man in his late twenties. He introduced himself as Alonso. Between my broken Spanish, his broken English, a pocket dictionary, and gestures (dangerously close to mime), we managed to have an enjoyable conversation. Developing a growing interest, I asked what I felt to be an innocent question:

"So, Alonso, what is your last name?"

A dark cloud formed over our conversation.

"Alonso, what is it?"

His eyes dropped. He mumbled that all Americans found his name extremely amusing.

What could it be?

He refused to tell me.

Having been born with a name I could never identify with, I felt my sensitivity would be greater than that of the average person. Placing hand on heart, I swore I wouldn't laugh. With the passage of time, numerous glasses of wine, inordinate begging and pleading, I eventually wore him down. He finally pulled out his wallet, and tossed his national identification card on the table. My curiosity was piqued as I slowly picked up the card, feigning complete self-control. Next to his photo, I read:

Alonso Penis

I doubled over in my chair laughing until my balance left me on my side. I looked up at Alonso, once again awash in betrayal, and was deeply relieved to see him smiling.

Before long, we were joking about what it's like to make a dinner reservation for:

"Penis, party of six."

And if the bank asks for his signature, Alonso simply signs ⚭.

Does a name really have an impact on one's life? Just try watching a jeweler engrave *All My Love, A. Penis* on a gold watch with a steady hand.

My parents, being of German heritage, decided to give me a German name—Gertrude. Certainly in Germany, there must be an abundance of happy Gertrudes in lederhosen frolicking in the Black Forest, but growing up in America, there were few role models. No famous actresses or beautiful models; only eighty-year-old Gertrude Flothmeir, the minister's wife. Later, I became aware of Gertrude Stein, also noticeably absent from the pages of *Tiger Beat.*

My self-image left much to be desired. I saw myself as a stout fräulein in a Heidi costume, with a stick and two pails across my shoulders traipsing down the hills to feed the goats.

In my early teens, I searched forever at mall gift shops to find my name on the racks of personalized mini bicycle license plates, key chains, and coffee mugs, but with as much success as a Hortense might have had.

> Later, I became aware of Gertrude Stein, also noticeably absent from the pages of Tiger Beat.

It got even worse in Spanish class. Where other names beautifully translate into the "itas" and "lindas," my new handle was, well . . . Hertrudis. I sat behind my hand-scrawled name-card feeling like a hairy tuber on display at the botanical gardens.

Eventually, after many attempts at nickname aliases, I sat down with a large extra-dry martini and a *Name Your Baby* book. For the sum of twenty-five dollars, I legally changed my name in a Phoenix, Arizona, court to Marlowe. Even the good-old-boy judge couldn't resist throwing in a few "Gertie" jokes.

Looking back, there were a variety of reasons for changing my name, but one consideration prompted my action more than any other. No matter how hard I tried, I just couldn't imagine any man at the peak of passion pressing me close to him, looking me deep in the eyes, and whispering in a husky breath, "Fuck me, Gertrude."

On the street, we are often asked, with some measure of regularity, questions regarding baby names. If, upon mentioning to the father of your child that you've always had a fondness for the name Egbert, you feel a swift kick in the side of your womb, it just may not be coincidental.

When a stranger hears a name without seeing the face that goes with it, he or she often comes up with negative preconceived notions about that person's appearance. There's also the danger that a person may grow into some odious name he or she was given.

DRAW A LINE AND MATCH THE PHOTO TO THE NAME THAT FITS IT BEST:

(Men)

1. Roland

2. "Mad Dog"

3. Moose

4. Tom

5. Casanova

(Women)

1. Candy

2. Penelope

3. Marlowe

4. Esmerelda

5. Gertrude

(HINT: Casanova is the dog)

If you drew a line from Gertrude to photo 5, you haven't been paying attention, and Marlowe hopes that you are personally cursed with the name Brunhilda.

I have six embryos in test tubes in my basement. I need baby names fast.

Paul
Kansas City, MO

We get this question all of the time. A few of our test tube favorites are:

Baltimore, Boomer, Buster, Chicago, Cisco, Daffodil, DeSoto, Euripides, Forsythia, Guadalupe, Gunn, Hyatt, Iago, Ignatius, Katmandu, Kierkegaard, Linus, Madison, Marcello, Nevada, Othello, Spike, Vegas, Venus, and Zeus.

Many parents choose a name for their baby months before it's born— long before they've had a chance to look at the baby, be with him, play with him.

Instead of naming your baby before you get to know it, mark a big *X* or a *TBD* on the birth certificate, then let your baby hang around for a while. Observe him. Does he look more like a future cigar smoker or a budding Greenpeace activist? No cigar aficionado wants to be cursed with being "Happy" all his life, just as hippie types tend to frown on the Thurston Edward the Third monikers. Let your baby's disposition and personality influence what you name him.

You might even solicit others' powers of observation to help you. We suggest you send out the standard birth announcement, including a photo, but with a space left blank for the baby's name. Include a stamped envelope addressed to you, and ask your friends to write down their name ideas based upon their inspirations from seeing the baby's photo.

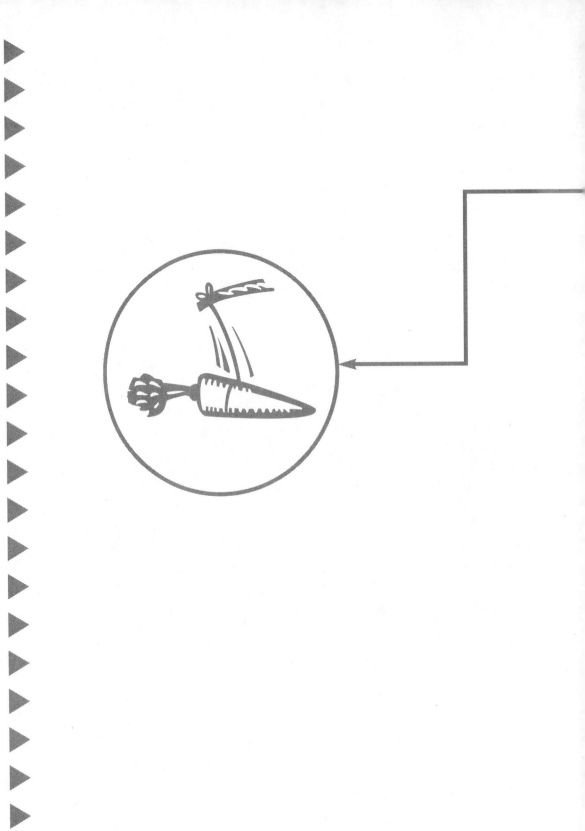

CHAPTER 3

Meeting People

All of the places you're *supposed* to go to meet people are actually all of the worst places to do so. In a singles bar, for example, even if you manage to successfully scream an attempt at conversation over the blaring pop tunes, everyone has such high expectations that the atmospheric tension escalates to something resembling the moments just before global thermonuclear warfare. Not exactly the most Zen way to make a stranger's acquaintance.

Branch out beyond bars and parties. Imagine the kind of person you'd like to find, decide where they might be likely to spend their time, then go there. Even if you don't meet the man or woman of your dreams, at least you'll have fun along the way. For example, if you love to eat, frequent your local "smorgie-bord" restaurant, and offer to share the last remaining chocolate pudding tart with the man in the Sansabelt suit at the next table. If you like tall men, you could apply for a job measuring inseams at Jack's Big & Tall.

When making weekend plans, keep prominently in mind the interests of the opposite sex. Women should realize that they are unlikely to find many unattached men spending their Saturday afternoons in the "Better Dresses" department at Nordstrom's. Moe's Sport Shack or Pep Boys Auto Parts would be much better shopping choices. Likewise for men; it is improbable that they will find many women enrolled in YMCA ice-hockey clinics. Coffeehouses in the vicinity of popular Saturday shopping meccas are likely to have a much better feminine selection.

Consider what it's worth to you to find your Prince or Princess Charming. Don't assume you'll get something for nothing. A twenty-five-dollar ticket to a benefit is not an extravagance. It's sensible investment in your future.

On the road to finding your true love, analyze your successes and failures and learn from them. Although you might not meet your dreamboat right away, take solace even in all your dates from hell. Every time you rule out another jerk, bore, or amphibian, you're moving your life forward. If nothing else, you at least know whom you *don't* want.

When you're on the hunt, be vigilant in all of your daily travels. You can meet people any time of the day. You may run into uncommon people in the most common places. For example . . .

The Grocery Store

 In the grocery store, hunting for produce is considered normal behavior. All the better if the produce is walking through the aisles instead of sitting on a shelf.

For a little fun, carry a black permanent Magic Marker when you go shopping. If you spot someone you want to meet, scrawl your name and number across the fruit or vegetable that resembles you most and slip it into their cart while they're pinching the tomatoes.

Music always helps set a conducive tone for a romantic encounter. You might bring a little boom box with you to the grocery store. But instead of blaring excoriating get-out-of-my-space music, try playing more "inviting" selections—for example, Mel Tormé, Guy Lombardo, Lawrence Welk, anything by Nino Rota (who wrote many Fellini scores)—and while browsing the cat-food section, you might opt for *The Best of Eartha Kitt.* As a strolling cocktail lounge, you can't help but meet new friends.

As you're on your way out, if you spot someone you like, offer to help that person carry his or her groceries. This can be an especially witty proposition if the person has only a tiny bag. And don't depart without asking for that person's name and phone number.

OTHER PLACES YOU WAIT

Make your chores work for you. Anyplace where people are standing still for a long period of time—the carwash, a movie line, the dog groomer, the post office—is a great opportunity to do a little mingling.

FREQUENT EATER MILEAGE

It's much easier to make the acquaintance of a seated woman awaiting delivery of her order of French toast than a woman running the hundred-yard dash after a departing express bus. Become a breakfast regular at a neighborhood restaurant, and hook into a whole new social scene. After other customers familiarize themselves with your face and your breakfast order, they will start to feel they know you. Seek dates, or just expand your circle of friends.

While waiting for your meal, unless you're attracted to a rapid eater, you'll usually have ample time to amass the courage to speak. Even if you do get rejected, you'll still get some *huevos rancheros* to keep you company.

If you are bashful, enlist your favorite waiter or waitress, who (after enjoying several months of your generous tips) will be happy to deliver your witty note or poem complete with your name and phone number to your crush after you depart.

When you run into one of your fellow patrons outside of the restaurant, you'll naturally have many areas of mutual interest to discuss. Speculate on the untimely disappearances of other regulars and mull over suspiciously mutual cases of food poisoning. Depending on how much you have to complain about, you may also want to share news of restaurants soon to open in the neighborhood.

COFFEE BARS

While coffee bars are more transient arenas than restaurants, they still offer myriad possibilities to make the acquaintance of interesting strangers. Frequent one or two coffee bars on a regular basis. After other patrons become familiar with your face, they are likely to make the assumption that you are not a serial killer, and will probably feel comfortable talking to you.

Coffee bars tend to have such a casual atmosphere that it's usually easy to strike up a conversation. To help break the ice, you might bring a conversation piece—a dog, a large ham, a Venus's-flytrap—and ask the person next to you to "guard" it while you run to the bathroom or go out to buy a newspaper. Be sure to thank them on your return and—depending on the level of care involved—you might offer to buy them a coffee.

If you do buy a newspaper, offer to read someone their horoscope, or ask for help with the crossword puzzle. While your benevolent side may encourage you to offer sections of your newspaper to your tablemate, if you're hoping to start a conversation, realize that most people buried in newspapers don't say too much—unless, of course, they're in the habit of moving their lips while reading.

ACTS OF GOD

Check out the crowd congregating at your nearest disaster area.

- Fires
- Floods
- Hurricanes
- Earthquakes
- Tidal Waves

If there are no natural disasters in your area, go to the bookstore and look them up and discuss them with other patrons. Or join the Red Cross and get free travel to the disaster of the moment.

CRIME SCENES

These are great places to hook up with people who share your penchant for ambulance chasing or amateur detective work.

TRANSPORTATION ARENAS

VEHICLE	MPH	LIKELY INCOME	TYPICAL OCCUPATION
Concorde	1,550	$500,000 plus	model, movie star, head of multinational corporation
747	625	$5,000–250,000	dog catcher to bank president
Train	80	$17,000–170,000	businessperson, anyone afraid of flying
Greyhound Bus	55	$20,000–100,000	gamblers enroute to Atlantic City
Public Transportation (subway, metro bus)	40	$500–85,000	homeless people to white collar workers
Tractor	25	$13,000–30,000	agricultural specialist
Riding Lawn Mower	15	$50,000	insurance salesman
Skateboard	10	$10 allowance to $23,000	teenager, messenger, rock band drummer
Pedestrian	0–10	0–$500,000	Occupations vary, if moving. If still, often a bum.
Rocket/Space Shuttle	Mach 4	rat pellets or up to $200,000	astronaut, nuclear physicist, lab rat
Flying Saucer	Mach 47	eight million zweiborgs	alien
Police Paddy Wagon	35	$0–1,000,000	felon

Sleazing along the Internet

If you own a computer and a modem, cruise the "chat rooms" on computer networks, like Prodigy, CompuServe, and America Online. Home in on the type of person you're looking for by joining a conversation group in a topic area that interests you . . . that is, if you are able to stomach room names like "Flirt's Nook," "Jewish Singles," and "Hollywood Tonight."

You can also start your own chat room. On America Online, for example, anyone can have a room of his or her own just by clicking into the "People" section, then "Available Rooms," then "Create a Room." Type in a room name, head on in, and wait for the explorers to join you. Name your chat room with care, so you attract only those who share your interests. For example . . .

People with Brains: when one wishes to ascend from "Where R U?" and "age/sex check," into actual exchanges of thoughts and ideas.

Conversation "overheard" on America Online:

Chat-er 1:

Yo!

Chat-er 2:

Yo.

Chat-er 1:

Yo, man.

Chat-er 2:

Yo!

Sometimes it's best to just avert your eyes.

MORE CREATE-A-ROOM EXAMPLES:

Fumbling to Ecstasy: How appealing.
Dog Fantasies: Bestiality discussions are always a big draw.
And . . .
GayM Locker Room
Short Skirt Stories
RelentlessWeevilHowl
Big Beautiful Women
WRU Wearing
Brag about Yr Wife

A FEW WARNINGS

• Be extremely careful about giving out your real name and telephone number and any other personal information. If you choose to keep your phone number a secret, realize that if you get someone else's number and call them, and if that person subscribes to the telephone company's Caller ID service, they'll know your phone number the moment they hear from you.

• If you do decide to proceed on to a real-life rendezvous with your techno-pal, realize that people often employ what could most kindly be termed "excess imagination" when describing their appearance on-line. It's usually safe to assume that descriptions err on the side of overestimated attractiveness. Nobody sends E-mail like the following:

```
From: Cyberella 9
Subj: My Physical Description
To:   Desklamp 3

300 lbs, with arms the size of small desks.
     Drawers optional.
Soon to be available at IKEA and other ware-
house stores.
                         Love, Cyberella
```

So, if you plan to chat with your computer crush in the flesh, you might want to get a photo first (hopefully it will be one of her) and choose a public place to meet with plenty of easily accessible exits.

BOOK SUPERSTORES

These bookstores, many of which are larger than some airplane hangars at major airports, and offer in-house coffee bars, are rife with possibilities for romance. Patrons are encouraged to sit down in reading areas throughout the store and browse through books. Many people stay for hours; some should volunteer to pay rent. In this environment, all of the elements conducive to meeting people are in place: people are generally sitting still . . . they're holding something interesting to talk about . . . something that expresses who they are and what subjects interest them.

In this arena, your reading material speaks volumes about you. Don't get caught making the wrong impression. Avoid amassing piles of self-help books with titles like *Women Who Love Too Much*. If you have a burning need to read such books, bury the evidence under your sweater until you go to pay.

THE OFFICE

Be discreet. However . . .

While toiling at a certain large advertising agency, we discovered that sometimes letting a little torrid gossip leak out can work to one's advantage.

We knew an account executive—the shy, Clark Kent type—who had a reputation for doing his job well, but kept a low profile. As the story goes, one evening he was working late, and his girlfriend came to meet him at the office. That night, the cleaning women were frightened by plaintive cries coming from the ladies' rest room. They phoned for help and our favorite security guard came to their rescue. He put his ear to the door and, fearing that a woman was in danger, burst into the ladies' room and discovered the account man having sex with his girlfriend on the sink.

Although to this day, "Clark" denies the episode, the corporate winds of fortune suddenly changed in his favor. Once the rumor got around, he was given a bigger office, better electronics than all of the producers, and was promoted to senior vice-president—almost instantly. Women who had never looked his way began to fill his voice mail with sultry messages. The old boys' club appointed him their mascot. By now, he's probably running the company.

SEVERAL WORDS ON BARS

If you're determined to go to a bar to meet someone, don't travel in a herd. You will seem unapproachable. We find it's best to head out with one friend—a "partner-in-crime" with a big shoulder to cry on—just in case somebody you're interested in rejects you.

If you're a guy, burn that book of supposedly surefire pickup lines you've got stashed underneath your mattress. Instead, just be yourself. Be friendly and natural, walk over and say hello. You might even offer to buy her a drink.

For a more unusual approach, send a little note to the person you have your eye on, via the bartender. In your note, be sure you ask for a written response. Just be careful that you point out *exactly* which person you're talking about, lest you end up with King Kong in lieu of Fay Wray.

THE SIAMESE PICKUP

This tactic works best when perpetrated by men, on women.

Two guy friends go out for the evening to the local singles bar. In the bar, they split up and pretend not to be together. When Guy One spots a woman he likes, he clandestinely points her out to Guy Two. Next, Guy

Two moves in on the woman. He behaves increasingly boorishly, in spite of protests sure to come from the woman. Then Guy One moves in for the kill. Like a white knight, he bounds over to rescue the delicate damsel from the loathsome beast who has been plaguing her. Naturally (unless she's read our book), she'll be overwhelmingly grateful to her "rescuer," not to mention impressed by his courage and chivalry.

A word of warning: If you get into a relationship with this woman, you'd better hope she's the forgiving type, when she finds out that "the boor" you "rescued" her from is actually your best friend.

I hang out with a guy who is very good at connecting with women. We meet a lot of women together, but even though my friend isn't particularly handsome or anything, the women always seem to like him and ignore me. How can I get my fair share of women?

Kevin, 33
Toledo, Ohio

Look at the bright side: You have a golden opportunity to study, free of charge, a master charmer demonstrating his proven techniques for attracting women. How does Casanova break the ice? Perhaps it's his ocelot-fur smoking jacket that gets women's attention. Maybe he stares intently into women's eyes as they talk to him, as if the rest of his life hinges upon their cocktail chitchat.

Over lunch sometime, you might ask this love *sensei* to tell you what he thinks are the best ways to pick up women. Or you could poll female bystanders to find out exactly what's so great about him.

After you complete your research, go out by yourself and try to implement his methods. Even if you don't enjoy the same level of success, at least you'll get first dibs on all the women.

I am a man in transition. I'm ten pounds overweight, I'm stuck in a terrible job, and I'm really embarrassed by the place I live. I want to meet new people, but I feel like

I should wait until I get my life more together. I think people will be more attracted to me when I get these areas fixed.

Roger, 34
Montclair, NJ

What if the woman of your dreams were to sit down next to you tomorrow? Would you ask her to come back in six months when you've solved all of your current problems? By the time you firm up your big butt, she could meet, date, and get married to someone else.

If you postpone living until you're perfect, chances are you'll never start having any fun. So instead of defining yourself by your problems, think of your life as a work in progress and start living in the now. Don't let a bit of life pass you by.

It may help raise your confidence level if you recognize that your problems aren't uniquely terrible deformities visited only upon you. Many people you'll encounter will probably be afflicted with the very same ones, or with ones very much like them. Already you'll have something in common to talk about. Moreover, a lot of people find a regular person "in transition" easier to relate to than a superstar with a perfect life who doesn't seem to need anyone to lean on.

I just graduated college and started a new job in a new city. I thought I'd meet a new set of friends . . . and girlfriends, but everyone I work with is old, married, and lives in the suburbs. What should I do?

Neil, 23
Dallas, TX

If everyone in your office finds the latest alternatives in arthritis medication more compelling than the latest alternative band, you might consider going back to college. Stake out campus bars. Even the old college libraries and campus bookstores are fun places to meet new people when you don't have a paper due at eight A.M. next day. You don't have to stick your nose back in the grindstone—just poke it in a few open doors.

MEETING PEOPLE: TECHNIQUES

WRONG NUMBERS

If you like the way your caller sounds, keep talking.

BLIND DATE SWAPPING

In old-school blind dating, you have very little recourse if a so-called friend sets you up with the long-lost twin sister of the Hydra.

Try our blind dating concept that comes with a guarantee. Blind Date Swapping! Trade dates like baseball cards—with all your friends.

Your address book is probably chock full of perfectly normal, desirable, attractive men and women with all the essential qualities. For some reason, you just never "clicked" with them romantically. Consider these people a valuable commodity. Pass your surplus stock on to qualified friends! In return, these friends should provide you with their eligible castoffs. Just remember . . .

Give as good as you wish to get.

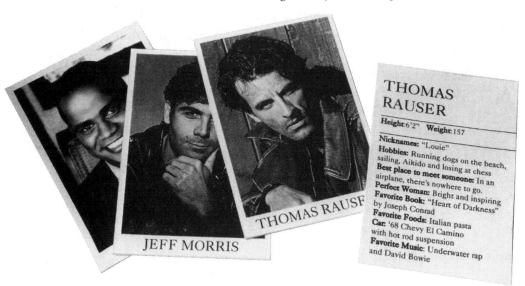

JEFF MORRIS

THOMAS RAUSE

THOMAS RAUSER

Height: 6'2"   Weight: 157

Nicknames: "Louie"
Hobbies: Running dogs on the beach, sailing, Aikido and losing at chess
Best place to meet someone: In an airplane, there's nowhere to go.
Perfect Woman: Bright and inspiring
Favorite Book: "Heart of Darkness" by Joseph Conrad
Favorite Foods: Italian pasta
Car: '68 Chevy El Camino with hot rod suspension
Favorite Music: Underwater rap and David Bowie

Trade 'em, swap 'em . . . collect the whole series!

SUNDAY BRUNCH

This is a great way to meet new dates and friends.

Invite eight different interesting people who don't know each other to Sunday brunch at a fun restaurant (so you don't have to cook, clean up, or pay for anyone but yourself). Or invite four people and ask them each to bring someone of the opposite sex. It's more fun if the invitees don't know each other, but have something in common to talk about.

This is a great excuse to make contact with some stranger who catches your eye. Approach him and say something like "You know, I put together a fabulous brunch on Sundays at a restaurant for eight interesting people who have never met each other before." (Describe some of your more compelling guests.) "You look like fun. I'd love to invite you." Such flattery rarely fails.

Don't forget to ask for your new friend's phone number and call him, as well as all of your other guests, to remind them the day before your brunch and to confirm their attendance. Be sure to choose a restaurant that takes reservations, and have them hold a big table for you and your new circle of friends.

GOOD DEEDS

Offer to walk the firemen's dalmatian or ask cute men if you can help them cross the street. If you have an attractive neighbor, when you're going shopping, ask him if he needs anything from the store. Bring him a piece of the huge cake you just baked.

If you need a little assistance, small tasks, such as opening your tightly sealed Coke bottle at lunch every day, can be used as a method to meet one new person each lunch hour. Look around for a good-looking guy with nice arm muscles, ask him to open it for you, and explain, ". . . Because you look like you can."

THE ONES THAT GOT AWAY

Stay friends with people you liked who got married to someone else. Remember, there's a high divorce rate. Be there for them to cry on your shoulder . . . and later they just may fall into your lap.

THE PARTY LINE

Create a telephone and fax network among friends and co-workers from various social stomping grounds to exchange information about hot parties and happenings. Unless you're invited to an intimate dinner, don't be too worried about encouraging your friends to come, as long as they are paper trained and have kicked the need to share with the world the miracles of twelve-step recovery.

In fact, most party-throwers will be happy to fill the room with a few more friendly, attractive faces, thus broadening their social circle and compensating for those nasty no-shows. If you're crashing, just bring a nice bottle of wine and present it to the host at the door. Distracted by your generosity and good manners, the host may forget to notice that he has never seen you before in his life. Should he ask from whence you came, just make up a name—tell him you're a good friend of their good friend Bubba . . . or a relative of the Count . . . whichever sounds most plausible in your social circle.

THE CONGA LINE

You're out for drinks with a group of friends. You spot someone interesting who's drinking alone. Invite that person to join you and your friends for dinner or drinks elsewhere, and move on to the next location together. Pick up other fun candidates on your way.

RECRUITMENT ADVERTISING

Got five or six lonely friends of the same sex? Band together and run an ad in your community newspaper. For example:

> Six beautiful, interesting creative women seek boyfriends. Apply in person, the Twilight Room, N. Lafayette at Lincoln Boulevard, Monday, October 3, 7:00 P.M.–9:00 P.M. Please bring own hair and teeth.

It's wise to warn the bar in advance. Perhaps they'll even offer to serve discount drinks and free appetizers. At the bar, should you attract one of the Seven Dwarfs, just claim you aren't one of the advertisers.

RECYCLE YOUR OLD LOVES

Times change. People change. Sometimes they even grow up. Yesterday's "No way!" could turn into tomorrow's "Maybe."

WARNING!

Do not try to meet people at The Forum, Lifespring, or other weird gatherings—especially the groups that have one hand in your wallet while encouraging you to be more assertive. If you were lucky, as a child, you may have actually experienced their tactics free of charge! Many parents were more than amenable to locking their children in their bedrooms, refusing to let them go to the bathroom, and humiliating them in front of large crowds of people (malls, restaurants, religious establishments). If that's your background, it's probably time to move on.

PROPS

Carry an irresistible conversation piece that begs for attention from strangers.

FUR

Men become extremely approachable when accompanied by an adorable puppy. In fact, while walking an especially cute dog—a baby basset hound, for example—you may have to fight the women off with his fetch stick. You might also enlist your dog's assistance—to the best of his breed's abilities—in your attempt to meet new women. For example, if you're a man who owns a hunting dog, consider training him to track down women wearing a perfume that you find sexy.

If you are among the dogless, inform your dog-owning neighbors that you are available for free dog walking, and puppies by the dozen will come scratching at your door—perhaps accompanied by their attractive owners. Or volunteer to walk dogs up for adoption at your neighborhood humane society—where you may very well run into attractive dog lovers of the opposite sex.

To further increase your "animal magnetism," dress the little guy up. For boy dogs, go for a simple red bandanna or a tiny weight-lifting sweatshirt. Girl dogs look cute and elegant in a strand of faux pearls and an oversize satin bow. Or go all out. If you're a motorcycle guy, get your dog a puppy-size leather jacket. Even the most standoffish women will swarm around your dog, and will feel completely at ease talking to you about your pet and his trendy wardrobe. Answer their questions, then turn the conversation toward the larger mammals at hand.

Some pets are better than others at attracting the opposite sex.

ELECTRONICS

It is prudent for the woman in search of a significant other to purchase the latest in electronic wizardry. Using one's battery-powered notebook computer in a café is almost an ironclad guarantee that you will meet one, if not several, men, whose overwhelming shyness around women magically dissipates in the face of cool new electronics. Don't assume a bigger appliance will get you better men. You will not have more success if you tow a Univac to the corner bistro.

THE LASER

For those with a decent budget, a laser pointer (it looks like a small flashlight, about a hundred dollars at Macy's) can be a handy device to stimulate conversation. Not only can you use it to introduce yourself at close range, but it is also an effective way of sending a greeting long distance.

The three of us were at a summer rooftop party where we witnessed a demonstration from a man who had recently become the proud owner of this device. A few roofs away, another party was in progress. Rather than pulling out a bullhorn and screaming, "Hello! . . . Anybody interesting over there?!!" the man pointed his laser at the distant group of people talking. "Watch this," he said, as the red dots flitted across the backs of the crowd. One guy noticed the "target" on his friend's back and the entire group threw their arms up in the air, apparently expecting a bullet to follow. Lucky for us, this group of partygoers was not armed with semiautomatics.

Delighted with his results, the laser owner then moved his light show down a few floors, to the open window of a brightly illuminated apartment. A naked man who had just gotten out of the shower was crossing his bedroom to get a towel. He paused and glanced down behind him, saw the glowing red dot on his butt, and fled back into the bathroom in horror.

While this gentleman with the laser pointer appeared to be more interested in terrorizing people than introducing himself to them, this tool, when used in a friendly way, can light your way to "Hello." At the very least, it suggests that you have enough discretionary income to spend on frivolous items, and are thus unlikely to ask your date to split a two-dollar taxi fare.

GIFTS OF FOOD AND DRINK

If you're in a bar or restaurant and you spot someone you like, send them a drink or dessert; something sexy and appealing. And try not to send it over with a waiter or a waitress who's better looking than you are.

MAGNETIC FASHION ACCESSORIES

For both men and women, wearing or carrying attention-getting accessories is akin to being trailed down the street by a movie premiere spotlight and a pack of reporters. Your wearable props speak for you; *Approach me,* they say. *Ask me a question.*

HATS

Women who have limited funds to put toward their wardrobe should invest in a fabulous hat. A hat has special powers to transform even the dullest outfit into something special and alluring. Hats also incite men's imaginations. A big, glamorous straw number with a wide brim conjures up misty visions of Audrey Hepburn on a Riviera holiday. An elegant, net-veiled cloche has miraculous rejuvenative powers over men, jump-starting rusty manners and dredging up long-lost chivalry. But women needn't run out in search of a coffee-table-sized wide-brim or a black velvet bedouin headdress to get noticed. Strange and wonderful things happen to a woman wearing even the simplest simple straw boater topped with a couple of flowers. In fact, we've found from experience that women wearing hats usually get better seats on planes, special service at hardware stores, and choice tables at crowded restaurants.

Strangely, however, in our opinion, men who opt for antique hats need to use more discretion. Some men in fedoras look the part of the greasy hustler left behind after a B film-noir shoot. And as for the ubiquitous baseball hat . . . women often assume that men who wear baseball hats from dawn to dusk do so because they have something to hide—or perhaps not enough of it.

If you don't feel like a hat person, try wearing or carrying some attention-grabbing item that shows off your subtly stunning sense of humor. Just make sure that your prop inspires them to laugh *with* you, not *at* you. Avoid novelty accessories that emit little electric shocks or squirting flowers that cause small-scale water damage to your potential beloved. It is a rare soul who is able to turn the butt of a joke into a lover.

WILD TIES

Conservative businessmen, who may not feel at home toting conversation pieces like brass handcuffs or whoopee cushions to the office, can turn their business attire into free direct-response advertising to women, by wearing unusual ties. Conversation-starting neckwear includes wildly patterned ties, humorous ties, and ties that are copies of famous works of art, or appear to be. Joe, our friend from the Broome Street Bar who brings us iced tea on our Advice corner when the summer weather starts getting obscene, logged over ten inquiries about his tie one Sunday morning. The tie in question looked to be a bold Magritte painting of a hatted man that Magritte had yet to produce. Ties with multiple words or sayings on them are also successful promotional tools. Curious women who might otherwise be shy or act standoffish are suddenly compelled to snuggle up to total strangers just to get a good reading position.

SEEING DOUBLE

If you're a conservative guy, when you're planning to go out with another guy friend after work, wear the same suits—exactly—down to your shirt, tie, shoes, and socks. Women who encounter you will be puzzled and charmed, and most likely will not be able to pass you by without stopping you and asking you a dozen questions to satisfy their curiosity. Best of all, they'll probably laugh. And if you can make a woman laugh, you're usually on the right track.

CLOTHING

Many men, like raccoons, are drawn to shiny objects. On women, long, flashing gemstone earrings, full-length satin, sequins, and lamé have always been big eye-catchers. On casual occasions when you hope to attract male eyes, you might inject intermittent bits of sparkle into your attire. (We do not, however, advocate the wearing of sequin-appliquéd cat T-shirts.)

Tactile clothing items—garments that men long to touch, such as fuzzy sweaters, brushed silk, and soft velvet—are also big favorites. Men are especially attracted to clothes that seem designed to be played with, such as sweaters with pom-poms, fringe, or beads sewed onto them.

Like women, who often dress to compete with other women, many men often make the mistake of dressing as if they were most interested in attracting other men. Such men are usually garbed head to toe in sports team logos—often wearing a panoply of teams in a single outfit. These walking sporting-events billboards bellow the message to most women "I have very little in common with you." To attract women, we suggest opting for word-free casual clothes that let *you* shine out from under them, instead of those outfits that scream your affection for the Cleveland Cavaliers. You might even go so far as to wear shoes that aren't sneakers. Moreover, if you're a man who longs to get a woman to pet you, one friend of ours notices that when he wears a brushed silk baseball jacket to the neighborhood bar, some women seem incapable of passing him without stroking his back.

FOUL WEATHER GEAR

If you live in a city, buy an enormous umbrella—one of those sturdy sorts that appears to be about the same size as a three-bedroom apartment. When it pours, head out in search of the attractive, interesting weather-impaired and offer to save them from their soggy fate. New York men have a golden opportunity at 350 Madison, the Condé Nast magazines building, housing *Glamour, Mademoiselle,* and about thirty other publications employing, almost exclusively, women. Equally golden opportunities are available in the town or city near you.

POINT-OF-PURCHASE INCENTIVES

Next time you head out to a bar or party, follow the corporate giants. Marketing premiums offered at point of purchase are sure to generate high awareness and repeat business. Hand out a key chain imprinted with your name and phone number . . . or a pocket mirror that says, *You Look Beautiful to* [your name and number here]. Refrigerator magnets, sewing kits, penlights, shoe-polishing cloths, and rubber jar-openers are other options.

CARD-CARRYING

Print up unusual business cards that break out of the clutter. Give yourself an amusing occupation or define yourself in a new way: "Freelance Goddess." "Day Laborer." "Sioux Chef" (for a chef who caters to a largely Native American clientele). Others include "Dictator." "Between Engagements." "Dinner Guest." "Social Arbiter." You might even hand out matchbooks with your name and phone number already professionally imprinted inside.

PHOTO: WENDY ANDRINGA

THE POWER OF ADVERTISING

I've just moved back to Washington, D.C. I work in international law, mainly out of town, so I don't meet people from D.C. through my job. I just moved into a big apartment building, but I don't know a soul. I want to meet some friends, throw some parties. Suggestions?

Michael, 24
Washington, D.C.

If your building is big (and safe), your people-meeting process can begin at home. Put up a sign on the bulletin board in your building that reads something like this:

PHOTO: AMY ALKON

CONVERTIBLES

Everyone wants to know someone who rides around with the top down. First of all, they can find you more easily because they can see you—with your hair blowing back behind your movie-star sunglasses to the soundtrack from *Wild at Heart.* Even if you're totally dull, you just look like a lot more fun than the guy behind you wearing the pocket protector, driving the Dodge K-Car.

"THE OPPORTUNIST"

by MARLOWE

I was out with Caroline on one of New York's rare balmy nights. We were headed toward our regular hangout—Raoul's in SoHo. Parked outside the restaurant was an exquisite sea-foam-green '54 T-Bird convertible. We peered into the car, cooing over the snow-white leather interior and the Raymond Loewy–like dash. Suddenly, a silver-haired Frenchman in his early fifties appeared from inside the restaurant.

"Your car is gorgeous!" we exclaimed.

"Why, thank you, thank you," he said proudly.

He introduced himself as Jean-Claude.

Caroline and I were dying to go for a ride, but he put his arms around us and escorted us inside to buy us drinks. Our friend the bartender seemed to know him, so when he insisted we accompany him and his friend to dinner at a French restaurant around the corner, we accepted.

At dinner, Jean-Claude and his friend, also a Frenchman, were completely charming (they paid). Afterward, we strolled around SoHo for a while. When it got late, I was having such a good time that I invited him up to my apartment for a nightcap. He insisted upon leaving his car in front of Raoul's where it would be safe, so we took a cab to my place.

As soon as we got in the door, he immediately shifted into seduction mode.

"Stand still and close your eyes," he whispered.

He dropped to the floor, began passionately kissing my feet, and continued to give me a full-body cat bath.

It was now very late (we didn't have sex); time for Jean-Claude to depart. After a long, romantic kiss at the door, he whispered . . .

"I have a confession to make."

Here it comes, I thought, in dread. *It's either a wife or scabies.*

He continued . . . "It wasn't my car."

"THE LOST ART OF LETTER WRITING"

by AMY

Expanding on the note-across-the-bar technique . . .

Marlowe and Caroline and I were having drinks in the Royalton Hotel lobby, a giant Philippe Starck–designed fishbowl for people-watching.

A remarkably handsome man, his golden locks cropped in the Greek-god style, parted the shifting sea of mortals and sat down on a couch directly below us. Radiating charm and good looks upon several rather unremarkable acquaintances in his company, he slipped a silver case from his Paul Smith sweater and tapped out a thin cigar. He struck a match and lit it, giving everyone in the place a lesson in cool.

Can I bum a cigar?

I just stared. Then I pulled myself together and penned a little note on the back of my business card:

Can I bum a cigar?

On our way out, I handed the note to a waitress, and asked her to deliver it to my handsome smoke-signaling friend.

Several hours later, my phone rang.

Later that evening, I discovered the cigars were Davidoff, and quite delectable. After several savory months, I was forced to kick my little cigar habit and move on. But every time a puff of cigar smoke wafts my way, I look back fondly on my smoking days and muse about the power of the pen.

FORM LETTERS

Although we are not big advocates of the form letter as a successful pickup device, we think this very original example has a lot of charm.

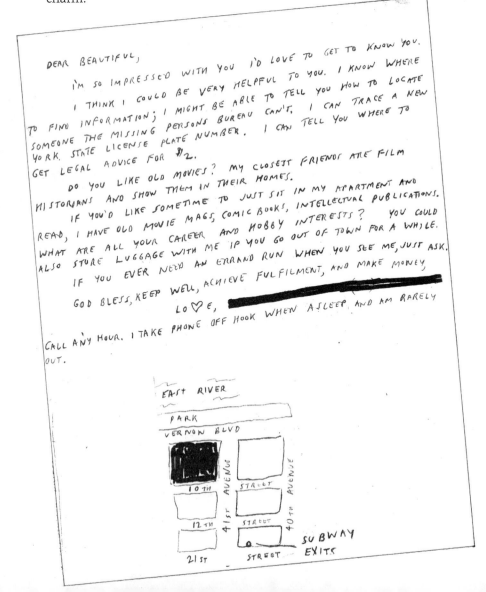

"WHEN MEETING PEOPLE BACKFIRES"

by AMY

Marlowe was in L.A. shooting a commercial. Flights were cheap, and her hotel stay was billed to the ad agency, so I flew out for a weekend of room service and left-coast adventure. I waited for Marlowe in the bar of her Santa Monica hotel.

Across the circular bar sat a tall, rather scruffy red-bearded man who resembled an elongated reproduction of Vincent van Gogh, eschewing absinthe in favor of numerous glasses of red wine. His face was concealed beneath a large straw hat. Dark glasses, a baggy khaki blazer, and *gloves,* even though it was the peak of summer, completed his disguise. I was immediately drawn to him.

For about ten months, we talked on the phone several hours every day. After we took a vacation together, I came back to New York, quit my job the next day, and moved out to California to live with him.

Little did I know that, soon afterward, he'd be chasing me around the swimming pool of his California bungalow in a vodka-ignited jealous rage, bellowing, "You betrayed me before you ever knew me!"—referring to the sordid things he imagined must have taken place way back at my high school prom.

I immediately began a series of clandestine phone calls to TWA.

> Little did I know that, soon afterward, he'd be chasing me around the swimming pool of his California bungalow in a vodka-ignited jealous rage

A word of warning to the newly unfettered spirits out there. There are tons of wackos running around. If you don't have the insight to figure out who's on the level, stick to your circle of friends for your explorations into the unknown. When you meet someone new to you, but who's known to your circle, you can ask for "references" on that person from those you trust. It's not totally fail safe, but at least you'll have a sense of who's going to wear the handcuffs before things start getting intimate.

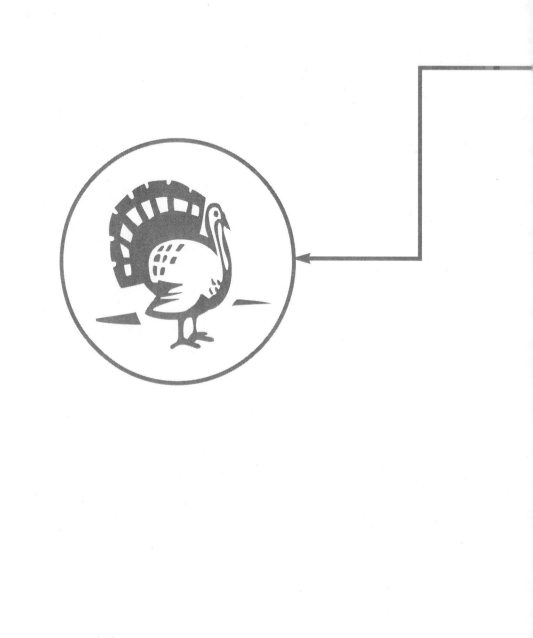

CHAPTER 4

The Personals: Looking for Love under the Used Cars

"THE GOOD, THE BAD, AND THE UGLY"

by AMY

I found out the hard way: The first rule of personal ads is that everyone is lying about absolutely everything until *proven* otherwise.

I answered the ad of a "Clint Eastwood look-alike." To my delight, Almost Clint called to ask me out. We planned to rendezvous in a SoHo bar/restaurant.

I squeezed through the crowded bar, choking on cigarette smoke, scanning for my stoic suitor. No Clint. Maybe he'd come upon a stagecoach being robbed on Park Avenue. Perhaps his horse had gone lame on the way and he couldn't find a cab.

Across the bar, beneath a furry hair mat, I spotted Charles Grodin. Or rather, someone who looked just like him. Why was he grinning at me? Moments later, he was at my side. Big smile. My heart sank.

"Hi, I'm Clint," he said.

And critics called *The Good, the Bad, and the Ugly* a long evening.

Ever notice how everyone who places a personal ad claims to be an "attractive, successful businessperson" who spends every well-adjusted evening strolling the moonlit beaches while listening to classical music, sipping fine wine, and asking the way to Margaritaville?

If this were really so, the beaches would resemble Times Square at rush hour and the grunions would be forced to throw themselves back into the sea to avoid being being trampled by the stampeding happy hordes.

However, in spite of the rampant hyperbole, personal ads can be a very successful device for stocking up on new dates; especially useful for those with hard-to-fill needs. For true fetishists, there's the ever-popular "Whatever's Clever" or "Anything Goes" category. For example . . .

Wanted: Big Bottom Gal
SM seeks female/females with large or extra large buttocks, hips, or thighs for bottom worship—I am very generous and clean. If your bottom measurements are 38++, please call. Big bottom girls ONLY need apply. Exotic times await.

Like acting school, a well-written personal ad draws numerous applicants, few of whom are qualified for the role of acceptable date. Be discerning in your culling-out process. Take all claims lightly—like, with a pillar of salt. Meet in a public place—such as Dodger Stadium. And avoid any establishment that you frequent; in all likelihood, you will run into your ten closest friends and enemies at the very time you wish more than anything not to meet up with anyone you know.

ADS WE'VE PLACED

These are a few examples of our forays into self-merchandising:

AMY'S AD

Tall Hungry White Woman, long red hair. Bikini-friendly. Tender-hearted. Mental Acrobat. Large Hooters, IQ. Seeking tall, extremely brainy cowboy with manners, integrity, courage. Bonus points for dog owners, rocket scientists.

MARLOWE'S AD

Wanted: ugly three-headed man with gout, Mensa.

CAROLINE'S AD

Seeking male raconteur who is not an alcoholic. Overstuffed-couch type body preferred.

HOW TO WRITE A PERSONALS AD

We suggest you write an ad that shows a sense of humor—that is, if you have one to offer. A clever ad that makes you sound desirable, smart, and fun is likely to attract at least a few desirable, smart, fun people. Unfortunately, you will also attract a good sum of people who simply *think* they are desirable, smart, and fun, but you'll just have to weed out the bad from the good. Remember that you are *selling* yourself. But be accurate. If you are a woman who looks like Ernest Borgnine, do not advertise a resemblance to Claudia Schiffer. Dashed expectations are never pretty. And if you've got bad news—rapid hair loss, for example—turn it around . . .

"More hair than Carlo Ponti"

. . . to entice your reader beyond it.

When you sit down to write your ad, first define who you are, then what you are looking for in another person. Mentally picture your intended customer, put yourself in his or her shoes, and figure out what words and phrases will appeal to that person. If you're only interested in meeting the literate, pepper your ad with obscure references to eighteenth-century fiction. If you're into factory workers, drop names of heavy machinery.

However, realize that ads which contain a lengthy laundry list of demands to be met by the respondent are a real turnoff. Such ads, which troll for custom-designed, pedigreed people who couldn't possibly exist, sound much more like help-wanted classifieds than dreamy quests for love and romance. Moreover, these ads say an awful lot about the authors—such as, "controlling, demanding, negative, and rigid."

Overwritten ads or ads that are clever just for the sake of being clever also tend to fall flat.

An Ill-Fated Humorous Attempt from Amy

Medusa seeks the Gorgon. When styled properly, snakes and lizards can be very attractive.

While this ad includes literary references, intended to draw respondents with a sense of humor who are likely to have picked up a book in the past decade, it plants in readers' minds the seed of suspicion that there might be some confessional truth to the Medusa reference. Consequently, Amy received only three or four phone responses, as opposed to 125 in a week for her "hooters" ad (for rather *obvious* reasons).

WHERE TO PLACE YOUR AD

Don't stop at targeting the person you're trying to reach in your ad. Also target them through your *choice of publication*. With the type of person in mind that you'd like to meet, browse through one of those big magazine stores to choose the right venue for your ad.

If finances are a problem, you may want to check out local papers, many of which let you place an ad for free as well as receiving free voice-mail messages from interested suitors or suit-tresses.

DECIPHERING THE PERSONALS WHAT THEY SAY/WHAT THEY MEAN

When responding to the ad of another, pay close attention to that person's self-description. Following are some of the code words, and what we think they *really* mean. . . .

"Strong, virile, handsome" = Hairy back.

"Not afraid of long-term relationships" = Can't even get a short one.

"Former runway model" = Airport location likely.

"Employed" = An unusual status for this person, worthy of media attention.

"Earthy" = Rarely bathes.

"Rubenesque, pleasingly plump, full figured, huggable, cuddly, shapely . . ." = FAT.

"Sculptor, artist, musician, Bohemian, aspiring writer . . ."
= Destitute. *You* pay.

"Spiritual" = Practices weird religions.

"Seeking romance" = Wants fuckbuddy.

"I like running, film, art museums, concerts, music, dining out, and romantic nights at home" = I am a generic human being who reads a lot of personals ads.

"Hip, yet moralistic" = Sybil.

"Have a lot to offer" = Have nothing to say.

"Wears clogs" = The need to boast about one's footwear says it all.

"Discreet" = Fuckbuddy.

"No head games" = I'm just angry because I'm trapped in the seventies.

"All calls answered" = Desperate.

"Nurturing" = Still breastfeeding.

"Creative" = Wishes he could trade ad career for movie biz.

"Seeks daytime relationship" = Fuckbuddy.

"Seeking model" — What "model" would ever answer an ad like this?

"Down to Earth" = Affinity for corduroy jackets with suede elbow patches.

"Enjoy fine dining, walks on beach" — Does anyone like bad food, bad weather?

"Honest" = Whining bore.

"Financially secure" = Expect prenuptial agreement.

"Educated" . . . Who isn't? In America, school is free.

"Queens resident, own car" = If there's one person on this continent who can bear my company, I'll be there.

"Seeks full-figured woman" = Fat fetishist, enjoys masturbating between the folds.

"Easy to look at" = You have at least an hour before you turn into a pillar of salt.

"Salt-and-pepper hair" = Father Time ringer.

"Seeking that special someone deep inside of you" — Talk about baby lust!!

"Enjoys talking" = No deaf mutes need apply.

"Grounded" = Thirteen years old, unable to leave house.

"Seeking stewardess, dancer, or model-type" = Brains would be too much for me.

"Secure with myself" = Has done est *and* The Forum.

"Cute and chunky" guy = Physique resembles cantaloupe placed on top of refrigerator.

"Seeks serious cuddling" = Mother deprived him of affection as a child.

"Exotic model" = Topless dancer . . . feels a little uncomfortable dating men from the office.

"Anything goes" = Does it with or without false teeth. You choose.

HOW TO ANSWER AN AD

Some people are still answering personal ads via "snail mail." However, after the telephone was transformed in the late eighties into a popular device for instant fantasy gratification—(even the most bizarre cravings can be fulfilled over the phone for those willing to fork over $3.99 per fetish-minute)—the main mode of response to personal ads also changed... from postal to Touch-Tone. Most personal ads sections now offer telephone voice-mail service. Voice mail is usually offered free to the one who has placed the ad, when picking up messages from respondents. The cost of answering an ad by voice-mail message is usually about half the cost of connecting with 1-900-TIE-ME-UP—usually a dollar or two per minute.

People responding by voice mail often think it's sufficient to leave only their phone number and a brief, gruff message.

MARLOWE RECEIVED THIS ABBREVIATED CHARMER IN RESPONSE TO HER GOUT AD

(In a stiff, methodical tone)
"555-2345. 42, 6′4″, 240, college educated."

This gentleman didn't even leave his name. How *inviting*. Remember, when answering an ad, if that ad is any good, such a response will be lost amid warmer, more amusing replies.

A MESSAGE THAT MARLOWE LIKED WENT LIKE THIS

(in a friendly-sounding tone)
"I'm Jack. I do have three heads. And I have three brains. I drink, smoke, and talk bullshit at the same time. No... I don't do any of that anymore... smoking and talking bullshit. I just came back

from six miserable years in California. I work in the theater, at night. I'm feeling extremely empowered at the moment. Life is wonderful, ha, ha, ha. 212-555-2345."

HERE IS ANOTHER MESSAGE MARLOWE LIKED

"Hi, I'm Mike. I do have a funny head. Actually, I'm hydra headed. I don't have gout, but I do have bursitis; does that count? My idea of a good time is scavenging dumps. Ha, ha, ha. I'm thirty-two, I'm a painter. I live in Brooklyn. 718-555-2345."

THIS ONE WAS FUNNY, BUT A LITTLE TOO CONVINCING

"I have three heads. I am ugly, I am stupid. I'm stupid, but I'm straight. If they had Mensa for the stupid, I'd be the charter member. So there it is: I *am* ugly, I *am* dumb, I have a number of heads here. Call me. 212-555-2345."

When you prepare to reply, try to avoid coming off as dateless, maniacal, desperately in need of sex, or as if you're rushing to create a family. And be yourself, because it's you the advertiser will eventually meet. If you do answer an ad by mail, you'll have a better chance of hearing back from the advertiser if you include a photograph (of yourself, not of the seventeen-year-old cheerleader next door) with your letter. In fact, many ads demand a photo in exchange for a reply. Make sure your response is readable (typing is advisable). And even if you opt to respond via voice mail, we still suggest you jot down a few witty, descriptive bits about yourself, and practice them once or twice before committing them to tape.

CHAPTER 5

The Date

How do you know if someone's interested in you?

Beavers thump their tails. Birds puff out their chest feathers. Monkeys stick their butts in the air. If only humans had some simple visual signal that would make their feelings easier to discern.

Although the signs of human attraction *are* numerous, nebulous, and confusing, there is a common denominator to all of them: *Odd Behavior* . . . displayed by those in love, in lust, or stricken with a high fever. The following are a few typical examples. . . .

WAYS THEY LET YOU KNOW THEY'RE SMITTEN

- On a dinner date, she asks numerous, painfully dull questions about your background, then stares raptly into your eyes, hanging on your every word . . . including such delicate pearls as "Could you pass the bread?"

- He informs you that he's really much better looking: "I'm usually not this fat."

- She invents excuses to touch you, such as minute-by-minute lint checks. Half an hour after the two of you sit down in the center of a very long couch, you find yourself wedged snugly between her thigh and the armrest.

- He meets you at a Saturday-afternoon matinee in a dinner jacket, tie, and cuff links. She walks her dog past your house in a cocktail dress, spike heels, and full makeup.

- Her life seems to come to a halt whenever you're in the vicinity. She lingers in your presence for extremely long periods of time, for no reason at all—while very likely missing job interviews, dinner engagements, and public transportation—in exchange for the privilege of basking in your aura.

- When you ask him something, he directs his response to your Wonderbra.

Ignore these signs and you may eventually find yourself flipping through the Yellow Pages in a panic, in search of the heading "Barnacle Removal."

How do you know when someone you like isn't interested in you?

To "protect" your feelings, people often avoid telling you how they *really* feel. Here are a few informative clues:

• When you ask her out, she says she is busy, but *suggests you ask out a mutual acquaintance.* Or she is always helpfully pointing out *other* women she thinks would be good for you.

• He regales you with tales about his dates . . . in gory detail.

• She goes on and on about the best sex she's ever had . . . not with you.

• In a potential office romance, he voices those tired old protests against mixing business and pleasure. He would do it with you at high noon in the janitor's closet . . . *if* he really wanted to.

• She says she can't sleep with you because you have "philosophical differences." True lust overcomes all basic philosophical questions.

• While he seems to enjoy your company at lunch, he will never, ever agree to meet you after dark.

• He overemphasizes what a *good friend* you are, and says that he could never sleep with you because your friendship means too much to him.

• She always comes up with mundane excuses for avoiding sex with you, such as eight-thirty A.M. emergency staff meetings.

• He makes eye contact with you in a really dead way—as if you're an aging trout—and, in public, continually looks over your shoulder for fresh bait.

"THE IDEAL WOMAN"

by CAROLINE

I was once hell-bent on winning the love of a demanding artist/intellectual type, who, despite my efforts, found me short of his ideal.

After I overheard him rhapsodizing on the powers of feminine mystery, I appeared at his next dinner party in a long black cape and veiled hat. When he asked how I was doing, I secretively demurred. I strove for an air of mystery. As I bade an enigmatic farewell, modeled on Greta Garbo's Anna Karenina, he told me that I looked like a witch.

I never even managed to get a proper date with him. But I often tried the next best thing: maneuvering him into a dark corner during the waning hours of a party like a Border collie herding sheep. Invariably, he would suggest I go home to get some beauty rest.

> As I bade an enigmatic farewell, modeled on Greta Garbo's Anna Karenina, he told me that I looked like a witch.

The closest we ever came to consummation was in several dances, in which I gyrated wildly around the dance floor to give him a taste of the sexual creature that dwelled within me, waiting to be liberated by his touch. As I mopped off the sweat after my free-form interpretation of "Y.M.C.A.," he informed me that I could considerably improve my dancing if I would try to find the beat first.

Months after I finally threw in the towel, I heard he had met the woman of his dreams. I looked forward to seeing who actually did stir his passions. As it turned out, "the embodiment of feminine mystery" was a hefty creature, garbed in a Redskins football jersey, sweatpants, and high-top sneakers. She greeted me with a hearty slap on the back that almost sent me sprawling, then turned to my former idol and barked, "Get me another beer, toots. I'm running low again!" As he sped off to fulfill her request, I heard the sound of someone falling off a pedestal.

Why doesn't he like me? I'm pretty, I have a great job, I dress with style, and I throw fun parties—that he always seems to have a great time at. And a lot of guys are interested in me . . . everyone, it seems, but him.

Samantha, 28
Anchorage, Alaska

A store near us had a sign: 97 BRANDS OF IMPORTED BEERS, AND MORE ON THE WAY. Yet everybody has *one* that's their favorite. Maybe it's just that you're a Tsingtao, and he likes only Meister Brau from Pic 'N Save. Finding someone attractive isn't about going through a checklist of their attributes. In fact, it's anything but intellectual. Sometimes there's just no explanation for it, other than that enigmatic "chemistry" between two people. Forget about him and before you know it, you'll meet somebody you like who also thinks you're just their brand.

What's the right way to ask a woman out on a date?

Hal, 23
Biloxi, MI

When a man wants to take a woman on a date, it's common practice for the man to call her up and tentatively mumble, "So, um, like, what are you doing this weekend?"

Understandably afraid of rejection, he's hedging his bet. But such a nebulous question leaves the woman on shaky ground. Is he inviting her out or taking census? She is likely to either tactfully plead that she has plans or opt for an envy-inspiring revelation, such as "I'm off to the Caribbean with Fernando," even though she's really weekending in town with Vidal Sassoon.

When you're interested in a woman, *be direct.* Present her with a definite time, date, and event . . . something fun she'd like to go to . . . with you. For example, "Would you like to go with me to the dinner dance at the Moose Lodge on Saturday night?"

If you're especially nervous about being so straightforward, remember that women really appreciate a guy with the guts to lay himself on the line. Even if she rejects you, at least it won't be for lack of a spine.

If a woman you ask on a date turns you down because she says she is busy, how many times should you ask again before you give up?

Harry, 25
Abilene, TX

Try to sense whether or not she's really busy, or is just engaging in an unwittingly cruel attempt to protect your ego.

If, beyond wishful thinking, you conclude there's a chance she may be interested in you, try asking her out, at most, two more times. When she turns you down or puts you off a total of three times, suggest that she call you as soon as she gets through with her peace-treaty negotiations, or whatever seems to be consuming so much of her time. Then forget about her, and move on to a woman with enough discernment to be interested in you.

He has my number. He said he would phone me. So . . . why doesn't he call?

Sally, 35
Big Sky, MT

Most likely he just wasn't interested in you, which is often communicated with a timid "I'll call next week." This is a cruel lie, but is perhaps kinder than saying, "I think you have all the personality of a one-ply square of toilet tissue."

On the other hand, maybe he is so shy that he is terrified to talk to you on the phone. Perhaps he intended to call, but procrastinated for so long that he feels more uncomfortable than ever about getting on the phone. Maybe he does call you, but doesn't speak.

If you want something to happen, call him. If he seems unresponsive, or always claims to be running out the door en route to Morocco, give up.

If you feel uncomfortable asking him out for a romantic evening, suggest coffee or lunch—something you can do during daylight hours. If you feel more daring, begin with drinks after work and go on from there. Alcohol and moonlight are the jumper cables of romance.

If a woman likes a guy, how often should she call him?
Jenny, 24
Colorado Springs, CO

Call if you want to talk to him. Just don't overdo it.

Because he seemed happy to hear from you once doesn't mean you should call him hourly to check if he's still breathing.

The same principle applies in asking men out on dates. Ask. Don't beg or call repeatedly for dubious reasons. You shouldn't give him cause to think he'd benefit from joining the Witness Protection Program.

"THE TELEPHONE CALL"

by CAROLINE

In spite of being a modern, allegedly "liberated" woman, I've always shrunk from calling men to ask them out. I know there are many women who feel the same way, but I've always felt it was a lack of courage on my part.

Eventually, circumstances forced me to overcome my reservations about initiating dates. I was obsessed with a gorgeous guy from the office, but after months of inner dialogue, I had taken no action. One afternoon, he stopped into my office . . . to say good-bye. He was being transferred to Delaware in two days.

I gave him a few weeks to get settled. On the appointed night, I brought home a jug of red wine, and proceeded to fortify my courage. A few hours and many glasses later, I decided to make my move or he would think he was being telephoned by a pervert with hiccups.

My now sweaty, twitching fingers managed to dial his number and I held tight through what seemed endless ringing. Just when time seemed about to merge with eternity, he answered. I quickly took another gulp of wine to moisten my vocal chords, parched by the recent enjoyment of too many cigarettes.

Suddenly, I realized I had no idea what I was going to say. I couldn't say, "Oh, hi! It's me. What's new?" because I had never called him before. I quickly scanned my memory banks for my own name, then mumbled hastily, "Uh, hi. It's—uh—Caroline. You know, Caroline from the office. You remember me, don't you . . . Caroline Johnson."

A long silence. I was once again painfully aware that the time I had just spent sloshing down glasses of red wine should have been spent strategizing. I was lost. My ship was sinking.

Suddenly, I heard myself talking again. "You know, autumn is such a lovely time of year, and I haven't gotten out of town lately. Why don't I just come down this weekend, and you can show me the local sights?"

> A few hours and many glasses later, I decided to make my move or he would think he was being telephoned by a pervert with hiccups.

I don't know how it happened, but the words were said and I couldn't get them back. I waited for his laughter and hoped that maybe we could be friends at some point in the future, after the embarrassment of this conversation had worn off.

After a long hesitation, he responded. "Well, uh, why not? Sure, come on down."

My subconscious took over to arrange the logistics, shortly before I passed out facedown on top of the telephone. The next morning, I awoke to the sound of my telephone receiver off the hook, and a hammering in my head that suggested an oncoming stroke. As I recalled the evening's events, I was dumbfounded about what had transpired. I wanted to turn back the clock. But I knew I had to go through with it, or I'd have to make yet another call to cancel, and endure last night's ordeal all over again.

> My subconscious took over to arrange the logistics, shortly before I passed out face down on top of the telephone.

Two years later, as he and I sat on the beach raising a toast "to us," I reflected on how it had all begun . . . with my fingers bravely dialing his phone number.

THE WAITING GAME

You're a guy out at a bar with a bunch of guys from your office one night after work. Suddenly somebody gives you a really good knock from behind—nearly causing you to spill your drink on your new boss. Annoyed, you turn to give Mr. Minnesota Vikings a piece of your mind. But the moment you set eyes on the perpetrator—all the way up her long tan legs to the top of her long wavy black hair—cartoon birds and butterflies suddenly take flight in your head and you forgive her completely for all offenses, past, present, and future.

You long to introduce yourself, to say something witty, but suddenly speech is a problem. You sputter out an introduction, and the two of you begin to talk. You have drinks, then dinner, then you walk her to her car. Just as she's getting in, somehow in your fog of love and lust you manage to remember to get her phone number before she drives off.

And that's where the problem begins.

The moment you get home, you run to the phone, longing to call her just to reassure yourself that she still exists. Luckily, the clock stops you. It's way past midnight, so you hit the pillow. The following are a few of our ideas to keep you, upon awakening, from doing irreparable damage to your heart with your telephone.

WHEN TO CALL

Once you fall into such a dreamy romantic reverie that crossing the street safely becomes a problem, making the right decisions about when to call, and how often, is understandably difficult—especially whenever a conversation about the latest innovations in wing nuts with the object of your affection becomes a thrilling proposition.

While most men and women insist that, in love and dating situations, they want people who are interested in them to be "direct," we've seen from experience after painful experience that blatant "directness" usually results in getting booted *directly* out of the picture.

In fact, we are convinced that people should guide themselves in amorous situations by practicing that time-tested concept that continues to have great merit today: Playing Hard-to-Get.

For those of you to whom this concept has remained foreign, what it means is, very basically, keeping your cool in the early stages of love and dating. Even if you are feeling anything *but* cool, you should give everything you have to *pretending* that you are. By so doing, you maintain your value in the mind of the person in whom you're interested and prevent her from taking you for granted.

Also, by conveying the impression that you might be slightly out of reach, you maintain a sense of mystery about you in that person's eyes, and leave them yearning to see and know more. Being scantily clad can be a lot sexier than going completely nude . . . as something is left to the imagination; likewise, a person who calls twice a week maintains an aura of mystery much greater than one who calls twice a day. You want the person to whom you're attracted to see you as a potential lover, not as someone who should be incarcerated for making annoyance calls.

Don't let your love object know she's on your mind twenty-four hours *per hour.* When you feel as if your fingers might just catch fire and fall off if you don't call, fax, or E-mail her office for the third time in one day, consider yourself your own worst enemy and take immediate steps toward self-protection. Either banish yourself from all areas that contain tele-phones, or if that is impossible, place your love object's phone number in a place where you have to stack several chairs to reach it. If you're an es-pecially extreme case, rent yourself a set of wooden stocks from a local theatrical prop house. Entrust a good friend in close proximity with the key, in case of emergency.

In spite of our suggesting these drastic preventive measures, don't be misled into thinking that you should totally avoid calling. It's just impor-tant that you continually keep the big picture prominently in mind; keep reminding yourself of your long-term goals. And before you rashly dial the phone one time too many, remember that short-term gratification usually makes for long-term regret.

The following is a little sample time line of telephone-call and date scheduling that is likely to convey "interest" to the one you are pursuing . . . rather than the truth: that you would like to Velcro yourself to that per-son's body as soon as possible. Take note that this time line would very likely be much more drawn out in some urban areas such as New York, Chicago, and Los Angeles, or other places in which people tend to be con-sumed by their careers, and often put their personal lives somewhat on the back burner.

WHEN TO CALL: A SAMPLE TIME LINE

☎ **Friday:** At a party, you meet a woman. Before you depart, you ask her for her phone number and give her yours. Do not call Saturday. Do not call Sunday. Make her wonder about you. Wait to call until early in the fol-lowing week.

☎ **Monday morning:** You call her at work and tell her what a great time you had talking to her at the party. You ask her out for drinks Wednesday evening, or for drinks and dinner, your budget permitting. (Asking her out for a weekend night—or even a Thursday night in many urban areas—would be considered "serious." It's best that you first ask her out on a weeknight, which is usually seen as a more casual night; both so you don't scare her off by coming on too strong too fast, and so you can get to know each other in a more low-pressure romantic atmosphere.)

☎ **Wednesday evening:** You go out for drinks right after work and end up staying out together till midnight. You drive her home, walk her to her door, and kiss her good-night, to the tune of the *1812 Overture* roaring through your head. You probably say something like "I'll call you tomorrow." If you promise to call at a specific time or on a specific date, be sure that you follow through and call when you said you would. That's always a big bone of contention with women, and failing to do so is a quick ticket toward a reputation for being "a jerk."

If you're still head over heels about her when you wake up the next morning (Thursday), and you think she feels similarly about you, you could call her that day and ask her out for Saturday night. Be sure you thank her for a lovely time the previous evening.

If you start feeling a little ambivalent about her, but you'd still like to see her again, you might wait until Friday to call her, then ask her out on a more casual date on Sunday afternoon; going on a bike ride in the park, going to the movies, or meeting for a coffee. Once again, be sure to thank her for a lovely time on your Wednesday date.

If you're no longer interested in her, you can either let the relationship fizzle out by not communicating with each other, or hint that you might not be able to see her for a while because you're going to very busy in the next few weeks. If she doesn't seem to take the hint, you may have to be a little more direct.

☎ **The following Monday:** By now, you should both have formed some kind of opinion about each other. Calls should now flow naturally between the two of you if you're interested in one another. Just remember to try to temper your enthusiasm—i.e., make sure that you don't drown her in phone calls—so you keep the relationship exciting.

How long should I wait to hear from her or call her back if she doesn't call me back when I leave her a message?

At any point in the time line, give her one more chance. Call her one more time, two or more days later. Although her lack of response to your call very likely means that she's not interested, don't leap to assumptions right away. Realize that stuff happens. People are busy, they write messages down and lose them, answering machine tapes *occasionally* break; maybe she had some raging dilemma one day that somehow obliterated your phone call from her brain. If you talk to her and you sense that she doesn't seem very enthusiastic, or if she doesn't call you back after you call the second time, give up. She's not interested.

It's really rare that I meet a guy I like. When I do, I want to call him right away. Why are some guys really uncomfortable when you pay attention to them right off the bat?
Josie, 36
Raleigh-Durham, NC

People who harbor some reservations about their self-worth tend to look with disdain, as the old quip goes, upon any club that would have them as a member—especially those clubs that appear to accept them immediately upon "application."

If you think you have a facility for discerning people's emotional makeup, upon meeting a person, weigh the evidence at hand and decide whether or not that person falls into the don't-like-me-too-fast group—and if so, whether or not you're still interested. If you don't consider yourself a great judge of character, to play it safe, you could act just a little bit aloof at first with all of the people in whom you're interested.

After a date, guys always tell women that they'll call them regardless of whether they will or they won't. I'm going on a first date next week with a guy I really like. If he tells

me, "I'll call you," how will I know whether or not he's sincere?

Jasmine, 32
Grand Forks, ND

Although there are no absolutes, you might think of his words on a scale that begins with the vague and moves toward higher degrees of specificity. In general, the more specific he is as to when he'll call, the greater his interest.

We surveyed a group of our male friends and came up with a few sample decodings. (However, bear in mind that just because a man is somewhat vague about when he'll speak to you next doesn't always mean that he isn't interested; he may simply be a sincere man of very few words.)

END OF DATE CLAIM ⟶ TRANSLATION

END OF DATE CLAIM	TRANSLATION
"I'll call you."	I'm standing here like an idiot and I don't know what else to say.
"I'll call you soon."	When the moon is in the seventh house and Jupiter aligns with Mars.
"I'll call you on Tuesday."	Definitely within the next decade.
"Would you like to have dinner next Tuesday? I'll call you tomorrow to confirm."	I want to have sex with you as soon as possible.

LOOKS CAN KILL

When you get ready for your evening, going to some trouble to look attractive is one thing. Making yourself look as if you just emerged from four hours of special-effects wardrobe and makeup is yet another.

Women should not reveal Victoria's Secret before the appetizers arrive. Men who show up in overly tight pants may give their dates the impression that they either have an Elvis fixation or an overheating washer/dryer.

In creating your outer image, opt for Bonding Apparel: a furry sweater, a soft silk shirt; *tactile clothing* that encourages your date to look at you and touch you. Once your date starts petting your angora sweater, it is unlikely that your first kiss is far behind.

Keep in mind that each item you put on may be exposed later in the evening. Early in a courtship, men should probably avoid wearing humorous underwear. Removing one's pants should not provoke laughter. Women should wear shoes they can walk in without assistance. Your five-inch satin platforms lose much of their appeal if you can't keep your balance without the use of a walker.

When styling your hair, take refuge in the tried and true. If you feel compelled to create a new hairstyle, give it a trial run the day before your date to test its moorings and the effect it has upon other members of the human race. And unless you live in a Big Hair Zone (Brooklyn, Queens, New Jersey, Texas, certain parts of the Midwest, Long Island, and southern California), avoid turning your head into a mushroom cloud in honor of your date.

In taming unruly locks, we advise against malodorous chemical holding agents and excessive application of "wet-look" formulas. Making a good impression does not mean leaving a greasy imprint of your head on your date's new couch.

Realize that your date will probably want to see your face. This rules out large-billed baseball hats, novelty beards, excessive use of pancake makeup, secret agent disguises, and the wearing of sunglasses indoors.

Photo: Jean Mahaux Location: Match

This is no way to camouflage a blemish.

On dates, many people seem to have great difficulty playing a most familiar role—themselves. If you replayed footage of one of your dates, would you recognize the person wearing your clothes? Your date asked *you* out; not some imitation of Madonna imitating Marlene Dietrich.

THE RESTAURANT GUIDE

In a screenplay, before getting into any of the action or dialogue, the screenwriter "sets the scene," with time, place, lighting, and ambience. A scene setting might read something like this:

INTERIOR, ROMANTIC SEASIDE RESTAURANT, NIGHT

When you're planning your date, pretend you're writing a really romantic movie. Pound out a few potential scene settings, and select the one that will serve you best. Take consolation that if things don't go very well on that special evening, on the page, at least, you can always kill your date off in the end.

The following are a few of our scenic suggestions for dates, gleaned from countless nights of horror and a few memorable evenings along the way. . . .

While romance is a very desirable quality on a first date, strolling mariachis and singing waiters are best left to long-term romances and festive funerals. Stick with the old standbys—moonlight, candlelight, white tablecloths, trees and flowers—all of which can usually be found in restaurants with outdoor garden seating.

When choosing a restaurant, skip those whose food might cause audible digestive disorders later in the evening. And avoid health-food restaurants unless your date strongly suggests one. It's hard to seduce someone with a cheek full of granola.

Try to pick a restaurant that makes you look good. Choose a low-voltage environment. Spotlights are dramatic, but they can have a blinding effect when directed on your date's bald head. Avoid harsh fluorescents at all cost, unless interrogation is a part of your evening plans. And if you plan to have a conversation or two, we also suggest avoiding those restaurants which have a decibel level commensurate with that of a metalworking factory.

PHOTO: JEAN MAHAUX   LOCATION: THE PRIME BURGER

Creative seating can make intimacy a bit difficult.

How do you feel about the idea that women should pretend to be dainty eaters? When you're on a date, should you eat everything or should you eat half and leave half on your plate?

Marcia, 38
Boston

Most men find it understandably annoying to treat their date to a pricey plate of grilled baby bunny *au beurre,* only to watch most of their twenty-dollar bill hop right back into the kitchen.

Don't be afraid to show your lust for life at the dinner table. Just try to pass up on the little extras that you might suck down if you were eating alone—the parsley *garni,* your straw, the marrow in your lamb-chop bone, the lemon in your Coke, anything that falls on the floor.

Your date is a microcosm of your future relationship.

WATCH FOR THE EARLY WARNING SIGNS!

- She flirts with the waiter.
- He talks to his own image in the mirror behind you.
- She keeps glancing over your shoulder to see if somebody better just walked in.
- He informs you that your choice of repast reveals your sexual fetishes.
- She splits dessert in half with surgical precision.
- He refers to the waiter as "garçon."
- She considers the dinner table a substitute vanity.
- He marches ahead, leaving you to struggle alone through huge, dungeonlike doors.
- She takes forever to order, changes her order several times, and still sends it back.
- She gulps down her food and then stares longingly at yours.
- He brings his cellular phone to the table and calls his director friends.
- By mysterious coincidence, her twenty closest friends show up at the table next to you.

If you spot any of these telltale warning clues, plan your escape route as soon as possible. The horrors will only escalate.

"A NIGHT OF VEGETATION"

by MARLOWE

This particular blind date may not have sported a white-tipped cane, but judging from the thickness of the glasses accessorizing his bald head, I'm sure he was forbidden to operate heavy machinery.

The only endorsement that he garnered was from my friend, his cousin, who told me that he worked as a "systems tester" in Silicon Valley, and that the two of us might hit it off.

I was wearing my standard sexy black cocktail dress. He arrived wearing a potato-sack shirt, Birkenstocks, and Sergio Valente flares.

"Hungry?" he asked.

"Yes," I said, assuming dinner to be part of the evening. Instead, he pulled a withered Baggie from his hip pocket and emptied some trail gorp into his palm. "I've got some dried fruits and nuts here."

After I declined, he gobbled up my portion as well.

The dinner course being over, I offered him a glass of wine. He consented and told me in between gulps that he "never touched the stuff," as it clouded his judgment. Before his glass was empty, a glazed smile crossed his face, and his clumsy advances knocked me to the floor. I pried myself loose, only slightly ruffled, and suggested we move on into the outside world.

He said he knew of an "artist's warehouse party," so we squeezed into his primer-gray Gremlin and took off. My worst fears were realized when he began maneuvering the streets of San Francisco as though he were piloting a mad mouse.

> I was wearing my standard sexy black cocktail dress. He arrived wearing a potato-sack shirt, Birkenstocks, and Sergio Valente flares.

He stopped at a corner store and emerged carrying a head of romaine and a head of curly kale. I assumed this was the course that followed the trail mix.

We pulled up in front of a house with blaring music. He strapped

on a giant leafy bow-tie, and informed me guests were to come as
their favorite vegetable. He offered to fit me with a curly kale bonnet,
but I politely resisted.

We were met at the door, by the host, adorned with a necklace
of carrots. He ushered us inside, introducing us to a professor from
the art institute, a bearded man in his seventies, wearing a lettuce bib
and jalapeño earrings. He rattled on about the Wiener Werkstadt
while experiencing a full two-minute attack of uninterrupted
flatulence.

We took this as our cue to venture elsewhere.
We ended up at a trendy after-hours spot. Once
inside, he was gone—but not hard to spot—as he
was the only person pogoing in and out of the
crowd like a spaniel in tall grass. After having to
pretend for too long that I'd never seen him before
in my life, we left the club only to run out of gas
on the way home.

> But suddenly, he dismissed the cab, and charged up the stairs behind me, leaving a trail of wilted lettuce.

We took a cab to my place, which I paid for, hoping to call it a
night. But suddenly, he dismissed the cab, and charged up the stairs
behind me, leaving a trail of wilted lettuce.

In trying to squeeze his way through the front door, he blinked at
me from behind his black glasses, and explained, "I have no desire for
a lasting relationship. I can only offer you sex."

This not being an option, I said good-night.

WHEN THE RACEHORSE TURNS OUT
TO BE A BURRO

What do you do when you are on a first date that's going really badly?

Sandra, 34
Sands Point, NY

Life is short. Leave.

A friend of ours once agreed to be fixed up with a man described to her as "an older Desi Arnaz." Unfortunately, upon arriving at the restaurant, she instead found "an older Herve Villechaize." The moment he set eyes on her, his thoughts turned to those of *amore,* and his traveling hands weren't far behind. Her thoughts instantly turned to those of emergency exits, parachutes, and getaway cars.

While some people favor a straightforward approach to get out of a situation like this one (for example: "Thank you. I really have to go now" or "I think we should call it a night") it tends to be entirely lacking in grace, and can often result in rather ugly verbal interludes played out before a large dining audience.

For those times when you absolutely cannot bear sticking the evening out, yet wish to resist the urge to inform your date that he bears an uncanny resemblance to bread mold, you might try one of these handy little prevarications:

"Oh, look at the time. It's been a really lovely evening, but . . ."

• "I think I have to go home before I start mistaking this white tablecloth for my sheets."

• "I'm on standby for the seven-thirty flight to Des Moines."

- "The security guards at my office are on strike, and we're all taking turns guarding the building. I have the graveyard shift."

- "The Mother Superior locks the doors after [pick time closest to moment of lie]."

- "I have diabetes. I have to go home and take my insulin."

- "I'd better drive you home now. My night vision isn't what it used to be."

- "I think I left the water in my bathtub running."

- "Did I tell you that I'm a volunteer fireman?"

"ESCAPE FROM ALCATRAZ"

by AMY

I was on a date that had begun to have a lot in common with maximum security. My companion had a bottomless supply of long-winded stories about himself, each one duller than the last. I clutched my stomach protectively while he recounted a joke in which the punch line was his zip code, and I wondered if it was medically possible to suffer internal injuries from excessive boredom.

> I wondered if it was medically possible to suffer internal injuries from excessive boredom.

Reeling from this torture, I began plotting my escape. I excused myself to the ladies' room. On my way, I stole out to the pay phone, called Marlowe and gave her the scoop. Ten minutes later, the bartender came over to our table to tell me that I had an important call from the office.

I went to the phone. On the other end, Marlowe prompted, "Just tell him it's a really big emergency on your job—then come meet me downtown at Raoul's." As my date watched from the table, I tried my hand at method acting, angrily protesting the injustice to which I was being subjected by my heartless employer. Marlowe, snickering on the other end, was no help at all in my attempt at turning around a believable performance.

After a generous display of manufactured indignation, I slunk back to the table and spilled out tall tales of a cruel taskmaster/boss and the night of indentured servantry that lay in front of me.

Sympathizing about my summons, my date uttered many dull words in praise of my dedication to my job, sucking the last remaining available air from the restaurant. Moments later, I made my final apologies and managed to escape with a few flecks of sanity intact, while preserving his dull but tender ego.

OTHER EXAMPLES OF EMERGENCY ASSISTANCE

BEEPERS AS PERSONAL RESCUE DEVICES

Many elderly people invest in wearable electronic devices to summon help in emergency situations. Beepers should be to the single and dating what these devices are to the elderly. On a date, when hiding under the table starts to sound like an inviting alternative to spending the evening with your companion, excuse yourself to the bathroom and call one of your friends. Tell the friend to beep you in five minutes. Remember to act surprised when your beeper goes off. Go back to the phone and pretend to call to find out what's happening. Return to the table, plead disaster, and grab your walking papers.

Flag Down Sympathetic Witnesses

One time, when Amy was on a particularly painful blind date, her date excused himself to use the men's room. As soon as he was out of sight, she hastily motioned the waiter over. "Nightmare date!" she whispered to him. "Can we speed the process?" Drinks, appetizers, dinner, and dessert followed each other in truly rapid succession. Secretariat brought the check.

Learn from Your Nightmares

When you're planning future first dates, keep in mind that a little smart scheduling can help you avoid being trapped for hours. Instead of making dinner plans, suggest meeting for drinks after work or for a workday lunch so you have a ready-made, concrete reason to split if your date is a clunker. If your date turns out to be fun, you can always cancel your imaginary postcocktail plans and party with your companion into the wee hours.

The Outstretched Hand: . . . Who Pays?

Dear Advice Ladies,

On a date, I never know what to do when the check arrives. It sits in the middle of the table, untouched. Should I let the man pay? Should I offer to split the check? What's the right thing to do?

Hilary, 32
Portland, OR

These are the current options:

He pays the whole check
She pays the whole check
You split the check
Or one or both of you end up in jail or in the back washing the dishes

We think the person who initiated the date should expect to pay. It is a vivid display of bad manners when the person who invited you out waits eons for you to kick in some cash. Decades pass. Species fall into extinction. And the check languishes forlornly in table center, untouched by human hands.

When it looks as if the staff is about to fax hostage demands to American Express, perhaps your date's arm slowly and painfully bends toward his wallet. After methodically recalculating the check three or four times, he painfully peels the requisite amount of dollar bills from his skin, lays them on the table, and bids them a forlorn farewell. Admittedly a horrifying experience. But look on the bright side. You've learned a quick lesson early on about how your date feels about money. Hagglers and penny-pinchers make for extremely unattractive companions, especially on a date. The check should be paid graciously—almost invisibly—by the evening's host *or* hostess.

When your date asks you to split the check, it's something akin to inviting people over for a dinner party, then passing the hat after dessert. A date should be an unencumbered example of generosity and good manners. To exhibit your own good manners, remember to thank your date for taking you. And be sure to reciprocate. Invite your date out the next time, cook dinner (a good solution for the financially unendowed), or pick up two tickets to something he or she has been dying to attend.

I'm poor and unemployed. How do I go out with women?

Get a job.

STAGING A SEDUCTION

Like military maneuvers, seduction requires careful strategic planning and great operational finesse. Surprise attacks usually work best.

"ONLY IN L.A."

by MARLOWE, about AMY

Amy, Caroline, and I were talking to a motorcycle friend on the sidewalk outside a Los Angeles café, when a vintage silver Porsche speeding by hit the brakes and screeched to a halt about a hundred feet ahead of us. "I'll be right back," Amy called out over her shoulder, as she ran up to the car, which I recognized to be her boyfriend's.

We continued our conversation, though our friend interrupted to draw our attention to the car. All we could see was a tangle of red hair and four hands flying as Amy and her boyfriend kissed passionately in the front seat. We watched as they slipped from view entirely for a brief moment, after which the door popped open, Amy tumbled out, and the car peeled out up the street.

> . . . a tangle of red hair and four hands flying as Amy and her boyfriend kissed passionately in the front seat.

I turned to Caroline and our friend and noted that we had just witnessed the first incident of "Drive-by Sex" in Los Angeles.

FIRST DATE SEDUCTIONS

If you've only just met someone, it's probably best not to rush right into peeling off their clothes. When you feel the temptation to speed up the seduction process, take care not to let the element of surprise cross the line into the element of shock.

"THE TANDY MAN"

by MARLOWE

When I was younger and didn't know any better, I went on a date with a twenty-nine-year-old Vietnam vet salesman at a Tandy leather store in Phoenix. What I was doing in a place that assisted people in bringing leather place mats into the world, I have no idea.

After dinner (at the mall), he explained that he needed to stop by the store to pick up something. I assumed that he was just trying to impress me by being important enough to possess keys. I browsed around the front of the store, perusing western belts with names like "Maif" carved into them, while he rummaged around the back room. Within a few minutes, he called out, "Come here, I want to show you something."

I expected to see him holding up a set of leather cowboy coasters he had just made. Instead, I found him standing in the middle of the room, completely naked, gesturing toward a "bed" he had just piled together out of giant, overlapping pieces of furry hide. His face (and the rest of him) revealed great disappointment as I persuaded him to put his clothes back on. Where could he have gone wrong?

"THE DINNER PARTY"

by CAROLINE

I was once invited to a dinner party at the apartment of a new acquaintance, who plied his talents in the plastic surgery trade. When the elevator doors opened, the floor was so quiet that I had to double-check the address. No, this was it, # 7M. Stealthily, I put my ear up to the door and listened to see if anyone had arrived yet. A few shuffling noises, but no voices. I decided to come back later, pushing well into the gray area beyond fashionably late.

After a bracing walk around the block, a cigarette, and two Tic

Tacs, I was back on the seventh floor about twenty minutes later. As the doors glided open, the sounds of laughter and ice cubes tinkling against glass once again eluded me.

I reconsidered for a moment, then decided I might as well go in. I knocked decisively to give the impression that I had just arrived. As the door opened, my suspicions were confirmed. But I decided to be diplomatic and not say a word. We could share a few drinks until the others arrived.

> . . . the silicone implants that lay like two jellyfish between the flickering tapers.

It was soon ten o'clock and he was uncorking the second bottle of wine. He had been regaling me with his favorite breast surgeries, occasionally making a point with the silicone implants that lay like two jellyfish between the flickering tapers. He seemed quite merry for someone who was being ditched by his friends.

Suddenly, he jumped up and announced, "Dinner time!"

"But aren't we going to wait for the others?" I asked. He gave me a blank stare. "I thought this was supposed to be a dinner party."

He leaned in closely, and in a bad imitation of Roger Vadim, said, "Darling, this is a dinner party . . . for just *you* and *me.*"

On a date, instead of focusing on how you're going to remove your guest's clothing in record time, your first objective should be drawing your date emotionally and physically closer to you. Begin by creating a conducive atmosphere . . . candles, fresh flowers, and dim light. Dim light, by the way, does not mean darkening the room to pitch black and burning a lone taper in a Gothic candelabra to prevent your guest from tripping across your bearskin love rug. Aside from making your sexual aspirations painfully obvious, you are also likely to give your date the impression that she has entered the home of the Addams family, and may, at any given moment, find "Thing" (you) crawling up her thigh.

We suggest you choose sexy music, and play it at a talkable volume. Following are a few of our favorites:

- Jackie Gleason, bandleader: *Music, Martinis, and Memories* (at vintage record stores)

- Miles Davis: *Kind of Blue*

- Les Négresses Vertes (French rock and roll)

- John Coltrane: *Ballads*

- Chet Baker: soundtrack from *Let's Get Lost*

SEDUCTIVE REFRESHMENTS

When planning the evening's menu, opt for luxurious, bite-size sensual snacks. Spear some of them on toothpicks and offer to feed your date a morsel or two. Sit down with your guest and relax. Don't race in and out of the kitchen with successive courses, as if trying to outdo Julia Child while fattening up your guest for the kill.

Avoid using your date as an opportunity to sing the merits of the latest fat-free tofu products. Your atmospheric theme should be "letting go," not "cutting back." You might even use the "forbidden" column of a diet as your menu guideline.

"DO'S"   "DONT'S"

BEVERAGES

all kinds of alcohol, especially good wines, port, cognac, Fernet Branca, and champagne.	wheat grass juice, chocolate Yoo-Hoo, carrot/parsley tonic, beers purchased at Pic 'N Save, and anything made with spirulina.

SNACKS

gourmet appetizers, such as marinated artichoke hearts, smoked mussels, cheese, and pâté.	beans and bean products, pierogies, kielbasa, schnitzel, and Dinty Moore beef stew.

DESSERTS

light sweets, such as berries with crème fraîche, and a variety of tiny French pastries.	any Entenmann's products (unless you're over sixty).

After you've laid your atmospheric groundwork, your next step is creating a bond between you and your date. It begins with conversation, which is your opportunity to get to know each other. This implies interest in what your date has to say. There's more to conversing than waiting for the other person to stop talking so you can get back to your favorite subject—you. Resist the urge to tell your whole life's story in one night. When you do talk about yourself, be open, as it will encourage a mutual level of openness from your companion. Whatever information you reveal, do not reveal it at great length, as putting your date to sleep rarely promotes sexual activity.

Once your date seems comfortable with you, you may want to sneak in a little talk about sex, which can often tempt your date into "the mood." Refrain from asking crude questions or making rudely overt remarks. Instead, subtly lead the conversation toward sexy topics.

Touching is another essential element of the seduction process. Find reasons to casually touch your date and to have her touch you. Come up with some pretense for touching her skin or her hair. Put your arm around her shoulders as part of a joke or anecdote. One of the oldest bribes in the world said by men to women is "Just let me give you a massage." While this idea may seem tired (to a laughable degree), it often works. Massages on dates almost inevitably turn into successful seductions.

At some point in the evening, it should become apparent as to whether or not your interest is reciprocated. If she keeps checking her watch, she may have another date lined up at midnight. Don't invest your best wine in this person. If, on the other hand, *he* seems receptive—for example, removing articles of clothing without you having to sneak behind him to cut them off with a scissors—you may assume your plan is working and proceed apace.

But if the hour is late and your guest is not responding to your overtures, don't wait around for the fires of passion to seize her. Your apartment will begin to feel like a bus station at midnight. Feign exhaustion, mumble about your busy schedule the following day, and fold up your tent. If you still feel you might have hope with her, reschedule and try again some other time.

SPENDING THE NIGHT

Keep these tips in mind when lust hits you like a speeding freight train. . . .

• Unless you are in the dental profession, avoid providing a selection of new toothbrushes for your nocturnal guest. It can leave your visitor wondering what color the last victim got.

• *Don't* keep a large fishbowl of assorted condoms next to your bed table. However, *do* keep at least one or two in an easily accessible area. There's nothing worse than the naked hundred-yard dash when the moment comes for the Trojans.

• Expect your guest to prospect through your medicine chest in search of electric nose-hair clippers and weird prescription drugs. If you would like to keep your spastic colon a secret, hide the medication in your sock drawer.

• Lose the toiletries from your last girlfriend or boyfriend clogging your medicine chest. You may still have fond memories of him every time you glance at that Royal Copenhagen bottle—and it will spark your guest's imagination too.

• Refreshments should be provided by the host—so your parched guest does not have to fall down your stairs at three A.M. in search of a glass of water.

• Avoid allowing your devoted pet into your bedroom to watch you have sex. Confused by your romantic entanglements, your pet may mistakenly sense a crime in progress and attack your lover with tooth and claw.

• Women's magazines advise using candles as a romantic enhancement. Don't, however, take this overboard. You may make your date feel as if he has to lay you upon an altar and pray for the miracle to happen.

• While in the act of making love, resist the urge to count "strokes" aloud like a drill sergeant. (A woman friend of ours who found herself in this situation worried what would happen when her partner hit a hundred.)

• Refrain from keeping stuffed animals on your bed, especially those of the sentimental, mangy variety. This puts out the message that you may prefer the sucking of thumbs to that of other items.

• The right sheets are very important. Kiddie-cartoon sheets should be left in the crib. No woman wants to make love to a man on top of Tweety bird.

• After sex, do not jump out of bed and immediately get dressed to leave. Most likely, you are not paying for the room by the hour. And most certainly, you will not be invited back.

SPENDING THE NIGHT FOLLOW-UP

Growing up, you were probably nagged to write a thank-you note the day after somebody had you over for dinner or sent you a birthday present. It's unlikely that anyone ever told you the polite thing to do when you sleep with someone for the first time. We think it's a good policy to always telephone the next day to thank that person for a nice time.

Even if, in the harsh glare of daylight, you decide the previous evening's rompings were a grotesque lapse in judgment, remember that even web-footed swamp creatures have feelings. While contemplating alternate routes through your neighborhood and bargaining with your deity of choice so you'll never have to see that person again, pick up the phone. You unmade your bed, now you have to thrash in it.

If you are especially anxious to avoid speaking to your close encounter from the black lagoon, lest he try to snare you into another encounter, be sneaky. If he is home when you call, hang up. Call back at an hour when he is likely to be out slithering through the tall grasses, and leave a message on his answering machine thanking him for a nice evening. At least you've been polite. Case closed until future insobriety.

Should you have sex on the first date?

The rules are . . . there really are no rules. However, we suggest one should never have sex *before* the first date.

HOW TO GET A GUY TO MAKE A PASS AT YOU

I met a guy I really like. We spend a good deal of time together. When he sees me at the neighborhood outdoor café, he'll join me and sit with me for hours. A few nights ago, he took me on a moonlit walk along the boat basin. Last night we sat outside talking until midnight. I'm pretty sure he's attracted to me, but I think he's shy and terrified to make a move. While I'm not *afraid* to make a move on him, it kind of ruins my fantasy about men. Any suggestions on helping him along ?

> Katrina, 32
> Manhattan

Since it sounds like he's interested in you, he probably just needs a little reassurance from you that he won't be rejected. You may be in for a bit of a waiting game. To bring out his hairy primate side a little faster, try some of these standard techniques to show him that you're interested in him:

Alcohol. If you and he drink, start with a few cocktails to relax him. Also, should you decide that you do want to make the first move, you might attempt to kiss him during an evening of alcoholic indulgence. If your kiss is not well received, you can later deem it something that "got a little out of hand" while under the influence.

Touching. While you're talking, touch him for emphasis. "Accidentally" brush his arm when you're reaching for the salt.

Proximity. The closer you get your face to his, the better. Leaf through a book together and let him feel your breath on his cheek. Refrain from simianlike behavior, such as pretending to pick parasitic creatures out of his collar.

Movies. Go to a scary movie. Huddle up close to him whenever the creature bares its fangs. Or, better yet, rent a movie and huddle up next to him on his Naugahyde couch.

Sex Talk. Turn the conversation to sex—even if you're talking about how a big spleen really turns you on.

Cold Weather. Forget your coat. If you shiver noticeably enough, maybe he'll put his arms around you. Snuggle up to him for added encouragement. Turn your air conditioning way up. Or, if it's winter, turn the heat off temporarily and blame it on your cruel landlord.

If he doesn't make a move on you after a good deal of diligent effort, reconsider whether or not you think he's interested. If you still think he is, and you're still interested in him, you're just going to have to wait him out. Be patient and persistent in utilizing the above suggestions, and the adoring beast will eventually attack you—hopefully while you're still young enough to care.

WHEN TO MAKE A MOVE ON A WOMAN

If you're a guy and you're interested in a woman, don't wait until the dawn of a new ice age to make a move on her.

We've heard countless tales from perplexed women who have gone out on a bunch of dates with men who seem terrified to even kiss them. If you're one of these men, while we understand and sympathize with your fear of rejection, realize that if you don't make a move, you will either lead a woman to feel that she is not very attractive to you, or that you have all the sexual aggression of a stuffed turtle. If you are dating someone, or meet someone that you seem to have a lot of chemistry with, we suggest you attempt to kiss her before she gets into the market for a Florida retirement condo. For example, the end of the first or second date would be a good time for a little kissing, and perhaps more. It might also help you boost your courage level if you look for hints from her (such as a great frequency of "accidental" touching), as detailed in the question above. Remember that if she wasn't interested in you, she probably wouldn't be going out with you. Besides, if you try to kiss her, the worst thing that could happen is that she might say no. At least then you'll know for sure that she's not interested in you and you can invest your time and your lip action in a woman who is.

WHEN YOU LOOK DESPERATE FOR LOVE

Quivering expectantly, the green-spiked jaws of the Venus's-flytrap lie in wait—hinged blades poised to snap shut on the first unsuspecting insect that lingers a moment too long in its vicinity.

When you are desperate for a relationship, that's exactly how you look to people of the opposite sex.

To the love-starved desperadoes, the most minor social gathering assumes the import of the Holy Crusades. They copiously scrutinize everyone who crosses their path and analyze each person's potential as a lover or a spouse. On dates, they dispense with frivolity and fun in favor of lengthy, terse inquiries about genetic solidity, financial stability, and life expectancy. Seduction attempts should, by all rights, take place in a speed trap.

If you're one of these hungry minions, realize that, even when you're trying to be discreet, your feelings are probably given away by the odd behavior common to the desperate, which is completely transparent to everyone but you. For example . . .

Dead Giveaways:

- Talking about when you want to have children on the first date.

- Trying to have children on the first date.

- Inquiring about medical history as if shopping for a horse.

- Stopping strangers pushing strollers to coo over their babies and sneaking glances at your date's reaction.

- Gazing adoringly into your date's eyes and agreeing with every word he or she utters.

- Breaking out the Billie Holiday albums right off the bat.

If this sounds like you, you're probably chasing a lot of potential customers away. Turn down the burners on your rockets, throw out the hard sell, and try a new approach: The Light Touch.

No matter how intense your level of emotional desperation seems to you, don't let it show, or all anybody you meet will want to do is run—far, hard, and fast—away from you.

So stop looking at every person who crosses your path as bait. Quit tearing off people's gloves to check for wedding rings. Stop handing out your business card while jogging, running for the bus, or chasing a purse snatcher, unless you are prospecting for life-insurance leads. And when you start dating someone, don't ask for lifelong commitment after the second or third date.

In other words . . . Be Cool. If that's beyond you, Act Cool. Once again, it's the old "playing hard-to-get." It still works today.

"BACHELOR SEEKS QUALIFIED CINDERELLA"

by CAROLINE

I had just emerged from an arduous breakup and was ready to launch myself onto the dating scene with renewed vigor. One of my co-workers mentioned that she knew a great guy who was also interested in meeting someone new. She emphasized that he was looking for a serious relationship with a long-term commitment. Within the hour, my telephone rang and I was speaking to my blind date. He was quite talkative, and seemed eager to get to know me.

He launched into a series of questions. He began with my place of birth, my parents' occupations ("Any siblings?"), and moved on to my extracurricular activities ("Any charities or community work?"), my education ("Hmm . . . graduate degree from Columbia, very good!"), place of residence ("Very nice area of the Village—that says a lot about you. . . ."), my state of health ("Ooooh . . . a smoker, but are you following a regular workout program?"). By the time he was done, I felt I had just been subjected to a physical by the insurance company and a background check by the CIA.

As you might have guessed, he was a college-educated, nonsmoking white-collar worker who divided his free time between the gym, his charity work, and vegetarian wok cooking in his Village apartment—when he wasn't interviewing women to see if they were qualified to go out on a date with him.

My instincts said "Stop," but my superego scolded me not to be so negative; just give it a try. As New York Lotto says, "Hey, you never know."

I endured several more rounds of telephone calls trying to agree upon a time to meet. Dates were penciled in, then cancelled, due to last-minute conflicts.

> My instincts said "Stop." but my superego scolded me not to be so negative: just give it a try. As New York Lotto says, "Hey, you never know."

The whole process had begun to really annoy me. I just wanted to meet him and get it over with. Since we hadn't been able to find a common time to meet for drinks after work, I suggested a quick lunch that coming Saturday. My suggestion was met with a prolonged silence from the other end of the line. *Quelle dommage,* I thought. *He's disappointed because he prefers the more romantic atmosphere of an evening rendezvous.* I was wrong.

"Actually," he said, "I was thinking of meeting you on a street corner. We could walk around the block in about ten minutes. After all, I always know what's going to happen in the first five minutes of meeting someone, don't you?"

"GREAT EXPECTATIONS"

by CAROLINE

One night, a few years back, I was out at an East Village restaurant with a tall, blond writer of recent acquaintance. He possessed that combination of boyish looks and the mind of a rake that women find so bewitching. Under the twinkling mass of plastic chili pepper lights, we talked books, film, philosophy, middle names, childhood vacations, the whole nine yards. I was smitten.

I took a deep drink of my piña colada. As I twirled its pink paper parasol, I contemplated my good fortune. Is it possible that such a handsome man could also be brilliant, witty, and just a bit bad? I was already analyzing which of his genes might be recessive.

Adrift in a sea of erotic reverie, I turned to gaze into his eyes. He glanced back, then spoke.

"By the way, you don't think this is a date, do you?"

The piña colada froze in my mouth. How presumptuous of me, I thought, a single man I just met calls me up, invites me out for the evening, wants to know all about me, and I boldly assume this would actually be a date. I must be a lunatic.

With a fierce attempt at gaiety, I exclaimed, "A date?! God *no!* Just friends, right?"

In a world of unisex perfume, women opening doors for men, and lovers who sleep together but are just friends, it's sometimes hard to figure out whether or not you're on a date. In movies from the forties, when a man asked a woman for her telephone number, he was probably going to ask her out. Whether good or bad, at least he had "intentions."

If you start by going out on what doesn't quite seem to be a date, you may eventually find yourself in something that is not quite a relationship with someone who sees you as kind of a pal, with whom to have some friendly, but not really romantic, sex. It's fine as long as both people want the same arrangement. But if one of the pair had something more intimate in mind, disagreements could ensue down the road.

If you are not sure what is going on, it's probably a good idea to be direct so your expectations are evident to the other person. Make it clear that you are inviting the person on "a date," or if you are the one being invited, make it clear that you believe you are accepting "a date."

After you've reintroduced the word *date* into your vocabulary, the person taking you out might feel so inspired that he'll get dressed up in his zebra peg-pants and borrow an 1969 Bentley just to impress you.

I'm obsessed with a man who rarely calls me—and then only late at night—and he asks if he can come over. I feel he really cares about me, but is afraid of intimacy. My friends say he is using me for sex.

Renee, 27
Little Rock, AR

Some people find the courage only late at night, after they've partaken of three or more cocktail parties, to do what they don't have the guts to do straight.

You are not his 7-Eleven. Don't pick up the phone at late hours. If somebody shows up in the middle of the night, don't answer the door.

Deconstruct the relationship and start anew. Shift the focus from the bedroom to the outside world. Return his call during business hours—the perfect time for him to ask you out to dinner or some other civilized activity that does not require rapid reapplication of "your face" at two A.M. He might surprise you and actually turn into a boyfriend. Or he will disappear altogether, which means your friends were right and you are lucky to be rid of him.

I feel guilty because I want to date other men in addition to my boyfriend.

Lorna, 20
Syracuse, NY

If you're not in a serious relationship with someone, there's nothing wrong with keeping the door open for other possibilities. You can meet other men for lunch or drink dates without anyone being the wiser. Getting a better sense of what's out there may even draw you closer to your boyfriend. However, if you want to go beyond drinks and snacks with another man, you should be honorable about it and tell your boyfriend.

What do you do if you are attracted to your girlfriend's best friend?

Mark, 24
Louisville, KY

Unless you are certain that her friend will be the great passion of your life, don't make a move, or you will set off on the emotional equivalent of Sherman's March to the Sea. You will lose your present relationship, probably break up a friendship, and if you change your mind later, the chances of getting your girlfriend back are basically nil.

I went on a date with this girl—she's okay—but after getting to know her a little better, I know that I'm really not interested. Problem is, all of a sudden, she's gotten really interested in me. She's calling me all the time and sending me little presents at work. Help! What should I do?

Andrew, 25
Maine

Very likely, if offered a choice between submitting to various forms of medieval torture or telling a person that you're not interested, you'll suddenly find yourself overcome by the desire to experience thumbscrews while "expanding your horizons" on the rack. As much as physical pain might seem an attractive alternative to the dreadful guilt feelings and emotional turmoil that usually accompany candor in such situations, being direct is the right thing to do.

First of all, you shouldn't feel guilty about your lack of interest. Your emotions are not something you can control; you cannot make yourself like her romantically or feel attracted to her. Accept your feelings, and try to protect hers by telling the truth—as soon as possible.

Leaving a woman hanging on a string, wondering how you feel about her, only prolongs her agony, and may even magnify her feelings for you. As in playing "hard-to-get" when you hope to attract someone to you, by seeming aloof or by appearing to be ambivalent you may actually encourage her to desire you even more.

So sit down and be honest with her about how you feel. The moment you tell her, she'll probably feel hurt and may get upset. However, the sooner you make your feelings clear, the sooner she'll be able to get over you and get on with her life. Telling her right away is the kindest thing you can do.

HELPFUL DECOY EXCUSES

The "But Mode" is a good tool for expressing disinterest in a person. It consists of a compliment about the person in question preceding the word *but,* and followed by the reason why the two of you should not be together. For example, "I'm really attracted to you, but somehow I just feel that we don't have very much in common." The words "you've probably been feeling the same way" are a good addition to the end of the above statement, as they help that person, even if she doesn't feel the same way, perhaps have a shot at preserving her dignity.

FALSE HOPES

Many people, in trying to soften the blow of telling another person that they are not interested, make the mistake of giving that person a few scraps of encouragement about future possibilities for romance. While they have no intention of ever getting involved with the person in question again, instead of firmly letting the person know they are not interested—at present or in the future—they make lame excuses about being too busy at work to get involved or pretend that they are still mourning some lost love. Such excuses give the other person hope that another shot at romance might come to fruition down the road. If that is not the case, make sure you don't leave any room in her head for dreams of the two of you riding off into the sunset together in days to come.

GETTING OVER A BIG CRUSH

I met this woman and I thought, *She's the one.* We went out twice, then she made it clear that she's not interested in me— not at all. The problem is, I just can't get her out of my head. Any suggestions on getting over this?

Andrew, 29
Baltimore, MD

In situations like this, your imagination is your worst enemy. Moments you shared with her hunting for a parking space take on near-religious significance. In your head, you roll and reroll footage of her face. All of a sudden, a girl who, in reality, looks a little bit like Miss Hathaway can start to bear a strong resemblance to Daryl Hannah. Before you do any more emotional damage to yourself, stop the projector. You're only making matters worse.

Getting over a crush requires the opposite approach to getting over a relationship. When a long-term relationship ends, it's important to give yourself ample time to mourn, as you've lost something that was a big and important part of your life. By languishing in your sadness after a mere romantic possibility sputters out, you give it more import than it deserves; making it all the more difficult for yourself to recover. In such a case, you're mourning the loss of what might have been—a world that exists only in your imagination.

Moreover, in such a short-lived "relationship," it's mostly your ego, not your heart, lying in pieces on the kitchen table. Every moment you sit around rewriting pleasant moments you shared with her into romantic epics, you're preventing yourself from meeting a new woman who might actually be a real romantic possibility for you.

So quit wallowing. Pick yourself up off the floor, get back on the road, and go look for a new woman to love. Ask your friends to fix you up. Make an effort to go to parties and strike up conversations with new women. Even if you don't meet someone in whom you're interested right away, as soon as you begin the process, you're that much closer to finding a woman who returns your affection. And, no matter how good your imagination, a rich fantasy life can never replace a real live person to put your arms around.

I had a crush on a girl I met at the gallery opening for my new paintings. I thought we really hit it off. She told me she had felt a need for more culture in her life, so I sent her one of my paintings—something I never do—and a long letter in French. She didn't even call to thank me for the painting . . . just muttered something on the phone when I called her about five days later. Where did I go wrong?

Carlo, 34
Chicago

You let your emotions bungee-jump off a cliff before you checked to see whether or not there was any water in the lake below. Although this woman might indeed have found you a romantic possibility upon your first meeting, when she saw your unbridled affection hurtling toward her at great velocity—before the two of you had even gone on a first date—all she could do was duck out of the way and run for cover.

Extravagant displays of your feelings are a lovely and romantic way to show your partner you care—*once you're in a relationship.* However, a woman who might be emotionally ready for, say, a first kiss, will tear away from you in a panic as soon as you give her the impression that she could be in great danger of getting licked to death.

Also, since you hardly knew this woman, showing her such lavish generosity so soon after your introduction probably made you seem desperate to her; the kind of person who consumes much of his time looking for love—forever lying in wait to pounce upon the first reasonably acceptable person in the vicinity.

When you're interested in someone, you might keep in mind this rule of thumb: Push too hard and the other person will push you away. Next time, go slowly. Spend a little time getting to know a woman before you messenger her your heart on a platter.

I met a guy about a month ago at a friend's party, and in the weeks afterward, I really went way overboard showing him that I liked him . . . a million faxes, little presents . . . that kind of thing. I'm pretty sure that he felt there was some chemistry between us at first, but I think he was just overwhelmed by all this attention from me all of a sudden. Will I ever have any chance with him?

Caroline, 25
Sun Valley, ID

Just because you're barraging the person to whom you're attracted with what we like to call "overly friendly fire"—such as hand-crocheted Smurfs and faxed declarations of love—it still doesn't make it feel to him any less like war.

After such siegelike pursuit, it's unlikely that the object of your affections will ever be able to see you as anything other than a lovesick crazy woman, the mere sight of whom will inspire sudden fantasies of foreign asylum. If you're a multiple offender in this arena, you should try to learn from the consistent failures resulting from such behavior. And as you take stock of the effects of this and other similar experiences, remind yourself to act like a human being, not a suction device, the next time you're attracted to another person.

In some rare circumstances, time can help your pursuee forget the fervor with which you chased him. It's unlikely, but sometimes you can win yourself a second chance. If you were pretty sure that he was interested in you at first, and you're still genuinely interested in him—not just trying to minister to your battered ego by winning him over—you can give it one more shot.

Let at least as much as two months pass before you try again. Then secretly enlist your mutual friend to arrange what will look to be a casual chance meeting. Have your friend throw another group dinner or group party, or plan a group brunch in a restaurant, to which both you and he will be invited. This is your opportunity to show that you've grown out of your mad-stalker costume.

Do everything you can to remove all traces of desperation from your persona. Keep the conversation light at all times. No painful reminders of how he didn't acknowledge all the gifts with which you barraged him. No recriminations about how he didn't call you when he said he would. Most of all, no drooling!

If it comes up, deal with the issue of your past "mental illness" with humor. Laugh at how you went overboard, and how he must have felt that he'd acquired a stalker. Then change the subject.

After talking with him for a while, examine again whether or not you think you're really still interested. If you are, learn from your past mistakes and play it slowly this time. Over a period of months, invite him along to other group gatherings, and show him that you're his friend. When he seems comfortable with the new you, you might begin asking him to do things alone with you; casual, friendly things like in-line skating, going to an afternoon movie . . . things that you do during daylight hours. After you get a good bit of friendship under your belt, you could invite him out for a drink or two during evening hours.

If he doesn't take some initiative from there, consider him romantically disinterested in you, and the whole thing a good reason to stay out of Hallmark stores the next time you meet a hot guy.

I just met a woman I really like. When we went out on our first date, I found out that she had just ended an eight-year relationship. From things she says, I don't think she's in the mood at the moment to begin another. But she's the first woman I've met in a long time who I think is really great. Is there any way to pursue this?

David, 40
New York City

There is: *very slowly.* If she's not ready for a new man in her life, don't try to rush her. That will only cause her to push you away. The best way to be the first in line when she does feel ready is by developing a strong friendship between the two of you. Do "friend things" together: see afternoon movies, go on bike rides, and share Sunday brunches. Remember, as impatient as you might be to land your first kiss on her lips, any evidence that you're pressuring her will probably send her fleeing. However, the more she begins to value you as a friend, the more quickly she may be enticed to end her self-imposed banishment from the world of love and dating. And, if you do become romantically involved in the future, this period of platonic probation could turn out to be a boon, as friendship is the foundation of a lasting relationship.

MINIATURE DATING

I work long hours and I don't have much time left over in the evening. How do I fit dating into my busy schedule?
Mark, 37
Los Angeles

Into a world that offers "quality time," drive-through confession, and the instant tan, why not introduce the miniature date? The miniature date is like an hors d'oeuvre; it offers the participants a small but delectable sampling of each other.

Ideally, the event should be one hour or less (travel time not included). To make it a relaxing experience, free from time pressure, the date should focus on one activity. Here are a few suggestions:

- Make a cameo appearance at a cocktail party or gallery opening.

- Share a bottle of champagne in front of the sunset.

- Get your palms read.

- Meet for a "dessert date" at a French restaurant.

- Go to a museum and ponder one artist's work together, i.e., the Anselm Kiefer Hour.

- Listen to Schubert's *Unfinished Symphony* together.

Should your miniature dating experiences lead to lasting romance, you might consider following through on the theme with an instant wedding (complete with paper tuxedo and disposable wedding dress) . . . rounded out with a forty-eight-hour honeymoon.

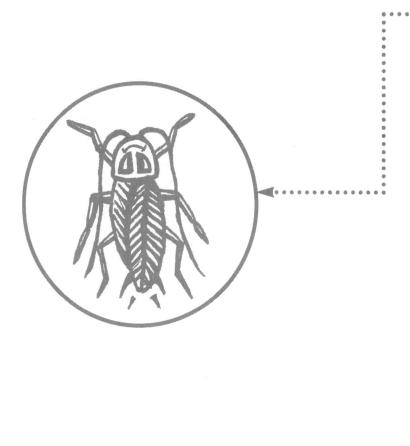

CHAPTER 6

Jerks

about twenty thousand years ago, a man wearing his best deerskin tunic paced nervously inside his cave. He had returned home from hunting several hours before, and once again, his woman was nowhere to be found.

He did everything he could to please her—giving her the finest amber necklaces, carving her face on his flintstone; recently, he had even finished a new cave painting of her favorite bear. Still, she just wouldn't stay home at night. He knew that something just wasn't right about the way she was treating him, but he would have to wait for the English language to evolve before he could call her his "Jerk."

A BRIEF HISTORY OF JERKS

The first Jerks probably came onto the scene as soon as primitive social life developed. Today, the species flourishes on every terrain, has split off into numerous breeds, all of which are noted for their stunning lack of moral conscience and savage behavior toward other species that express love and admiration for them.

The Jerk looms large in Western culture—chronicled in myth, ballads, opera, the novel, film, and especially, in the blues.

ZEUS WAS A JERK TO HERA

ran around with all the younger goddesses.

JASON TO MEDEA

dumped her for another woman shortly after she saved his life and his career.

HAMLET TO OPHELIA

drove her to suicide with many long monologues about his unresolved emotions.

MADAME BOVARY TO HER HUSBAND

humiliated her doctor husband by playing doctor with another.

LIEUTENANT PINKERTON TO MADAME BUTTERFLY

left town when she was pregnant with their child, married another woman, and let her wait three years to hear the news from someone else.

SCARLETT O'HARA TO RHETT BUTLER

toyed with his emotions while gold-digging and obsessing over someone else.

DAISY BUCHANAN TO JAY GATSBY

jilted him for a richer man, then she killed someone and let Gatsby take the fall.

IN *DOUBLE INDEMNITY* BARBARA STANWYCK TO FRED MACMURRAY

feigned passion for Fred MacMurray's insurance-adjuster character so he'd murder her husband, then she schemed to keep all the money for herself and let him take the rap.

MODERN DAY JERKS

These days, there are still even more species of Jerks running around out there; male and female. One type of Male Jerk we hear about is a guy whose undeservedly high opinion of himself is only exceeded by his undeservedly low opinion of the women he dates. He's a little fat, and he's losing his hair, but he has a certain boyish charm and that studied casual way of dropping the name of the Important Place where he works. After introducing himself, he looks deep into your eyes and weaves a web of metaphors that do not merely describe, but memorialize, your charms . . . all before you've finished your first glass of cheap Chardonnay. After a few dates, he finally flatters you into bed. The very second you're out from under the covers, his party manners fall by the wayside. In public places, he's always looking over your shoulder while you're talking to see if anyone more beautiful or more interesting has entered the vicinity. In a restaurant, when you go to the ladies' room, he gets up from the table to flirt with some other woman. While he is nobody's Gregory Peck, he endlessly criticizes your appearance, complaining that you're too fat, your breasts aren't big enough, and your wardrobe is sorely lacking. He treats you like you're a romantic stopgap, informing you that he's been unable as of yet to find a supermodel who meets his exacting standards. Your relationship is an on-again, off-again one, corresponding to his physical needs. He knows exactly where to find you when he wants to have a sex date at his house—he's much too cheap to spring for dinner—but when he's invited to a fun party, he temporarily loses your phone number.

One type of Female Jerk is "the Queen." Extremely beautiful on the exterior, she has enjoyed a lifetime of male fawning, and has become quite convinced that the world revolves mainly in her behalf. If you aspire to join her long parade of adoring serfs, be prepared to meet the financial requirements. Heavy spending will be in order, just to pass time in her presence—expensive dinners, truckloads of roses, trips to pricey events, and a continuous supply of extravagant gifts. The idea of sex as a mutually enjoyable act is entirely foreign to her. Applications for physical contact with "the Queen" will only be considered after ample contribution to the royal treasury. Her increment system might go something like the following: Spend $500. You may kiss the royal hand. For $750, you can undo a few buttons. If you would actually like to have sex with her, don't even dream of it until you spend at least a thousand dollars on her—and even that doesn't buy you much passion.

ARE YOU DATING A JERK?

EARLY JERK SIGNALS

- His smooth opening lines sound too good to be true, suggesting years of trial and error in singles bars.

- She dashes home immediately after having sex with you.

- He never pays for anything on a date, yet owns a large stock portfolio and a summer house.

- He has a wandering eye that includes your best friends, sisters, brothers, waiters, waitresses, toll-booth operators . . . and perhaps even a few overly fond gazes at your pet.

- He divides dinner and taxi fares in half—down to the penny.

- She withholds information from you under the guise of personal privacy . . . for example, she won't tell you her real name or home phone number (probably married), or let you into her apartment. Sometimes a person won't invite you to his or her place simply because they're ashamed of it—and usually for good reason.

- At a cocktail party his career changes as he moves from one conversation to the next.

- An hour before your date, from a restaurant, she bribes the bartender to call you to tell you that she's just passed out.

- He wears ribbed condoms inside out.

- You wake up the next morning to find her fully dressed, and your clothes folded neatly beside you on the bed.

- He takes you to a bar at which he's slept with half of the women— and they make sure you know it.

- She frequently alters her manner of speaking. In the presence of Brits, for example, she suddenly acquires what sounds like an English accent.
- The first time he's invited over to your house, he goes through your closets, remarking on each garment, ". . . Like this . . . don't like this . . ." to tell you what you can and cannot wear around him.

"THE VANITY CASE"

by AMY

The guy was almost too beautiful: thick, curly, longish blond hair, blue eyes, and Chiclet-perfect teeth. To round out the visual cliché, he made his living as a rock musician. But since he was also nice, polite, *and* persistent, I finally agreed to a date.

En route to dinner, he claimed he'd left his wallet at home. We sped back to his darkened "pad." I waited for him in the living room, a spare, tastefully decorated space, filled with modern furniture, a large, geometric wool rug, and dozens of beautifully framed photographs spaced evenly along the wall.

As my eyes grew accustomed to the dim light, I suddenly noticed something unusual about his wall of pictures: every single frame held a picture of him, in one sultry pose or another; about half of them, bare chested . . . and *oiled.*

I was too stunned to laugh.

He emerged from the bedroom. Something about his appearance was different.

"Do you think I should wear this shirt instead of the one I had on?" he inquired earnestly.

"Th-that's nice, too," I stuttered.

"Let me show you one more," he called, as he ran back into the bedroom, only to pop out seconds later, holding a large, leather-bound book.

"Here," he said, presenting it to me as if it were a religious offering. "You might want to take a look at this while you're waiting."

It was a huge, ornate photo album, filled with hundreds more pictures of *him;* faded childhood pictures, student IDs, high school prom photos . . . even a mug shot.

Instead of leaving me to ignore the huge volume at my leisure, he abandoned his wardrobe preoccupations in favor of guiding me through his life story—one photo at a time.

An idea flashed across his face. I could just tell it was bad from the glint in his eye. He slid off the couch and opened a stereo cabinet. "You can hear my latest CD while we look at the photos," he said, brightly.

"I think I need something to drink," I gasped.

"Help yourself," he offered, pointing the way. Images of his face tailed me into the kitchen. Afraid of what images of him might be lurking within the refrigerator, I gingerly cracked open the door . . . and saw . . . Myself!

There was a mirror in the refrigerator!—right in one of the little top compartments.

Staring into my own reflection, shaking my head in disbelief, I was reminded of a classic proverb from the annals of dating:

> . . . every single frame held a picture of him, in one sultry pose or another; about half of them bare chested . . . and *oiled.*

Never date a man who is prettier than you are, or who spends more time than you do in the bathroom.

ARE YOU IN A RELATIONSHIP WITH A JERK?

After you've been with someone for a period of time, it's easy to get brainwashed (by the repetition of bad behavior). You start to think the questionable behavior is "normal," just because you're used to it. Here are a few sample wake-up calls.

• You spend a lot of time together, because none of your friends want to socialize with the two of you.

• He claims to have dated Madonna and dumped her.

• Instead of gazing fondly on your lover while she is sleeping, you steal the covers in revenge.

• He uses his full name, including middle initial, to sound important when ordering a pizza or Chinese food by telephone.

• She disappears, returning with strange excuses like recurring alcoholism or temporary paralysis.

• He wants you to throw out your vibrator because it's bigger than he is.

• He embarrasses you at cocktail parties by unhinging his jaw and inhaling three chicken satay skewers at once.

• You worry that if you go out by yourself you'll run into her picking up someone else.

- He carries around an expired ATM card, as he has no credit cards or checking account for identification.

- Her friends hint around at trying to fix you up with someone else.

GETTING RID OF YOUR JERK

A Jerk is rather like a bunion. Initially, you might ignore the problem and presume that it will get better over time; possibly even disappear. But it doesn't get better; it only grows bigger, uglier, and more annoying the longer you attempt to ignore it. What once seemed to be fixable with a few doses of Compound W, when left untreated can require several rounds of painful laser surgery—which are not covered by your health insurance.

If you recognize the above Jerk warning signs, or others like them, in your love situation, it's essential that you take action as soon as possible to excise him or her from your life. Remember, the sooner you act, the easier and less painful the process will be.

Some people who realize they have Jerks in their lives are surprisingly reluctant to get rid of them. If you are one of those people, perhaps you are swayed by the impulse to try to make the relationship work. Maybe your ego has been through the meat grinder so often that you find it unlikely that you could ever in your lifetime get another date. Or perhaps your therapist is offering a two-for-one special on couples therapy.

To justify remaining with their Jerks, people go on and on about time invested, how difficult it is to meet someone new, how they're still attached to the person in their life and how hard it is to start over.

But if you're dating a Jerk or if you're in a relationship with a Jerk, just remember this:

Every moment you spend with Your Jerk is a moment you could be spending meeting someone new. So, go on! Give Your Jerk the boot! Then go out into the world and get what you deserve: a real relationship with someone who treats you right.

Why do women seem to be most attracted to men who are Jerks?

A Nice Guy in El Paso

A lot of Nice Guys are under the impression that women like men who treat them badly. Actually, most women dread the heartache that Jerks leave in their wake, but in the mode of bad boys from the movies—Marlon Brando, James Dean, Mickey Rourke, Johnny Depp—they long to be around men who seem to have a bit of The Rogue to them. Such men are challenging, unpredictable, and always slightly out of reach. Women relish the opportunity to try to tame—perhaps even domesticate—these wild beasts.

On the other end of the spectrum (the syrupy side) is "the Sensitive Man." While sensitivity is good, this guy takes it over the edge. "Love me! Feed me! Nurture me!" He's on a boundless pilgrimage to find a modern version of his mother. The Sensitive Man prefers "serious cuddling" to fucking your brains out—all the while calmly reassuring you that "he understands."

The solution lies between the two extremes. You don't really have to *be* a Jerk to *seem* like one. When you're interested in a woman, cloak yourself in the Rogue's air of mystery. Pull a shock of hair down over one eye, show up in ripped jeans and a five o'clock shadow, and snarl at the world every now and then for no reason at all. If you can't afford a Harley, at least invest in an old leather jacket that looks like it's seen one too many bar brawls. And always be full of surprises. Being with you should have a lot in common with riding a roller coaster blindfolded.

"Mommy"

PHOTO: JEAN MAHAUX

No woman wants to date a man who has to be burped after dinner.

BEFORE: The Nice Guy

AFTER: The Rogue

I've been dating this girl—she's an up-and-coming model—
and she gets invited to a lot of celebrity parties. She takes me
with her, but no sooner do we get in the door than she runs
off to flirt with the rich and famous—and ignores me until it's
time to leave. I've told her over and over again how much this
hurts my feelings, but she just keeps it up. I'm miserable and
getting more and more depressed.

Michael, 29

New York City

In spite of your telling her how her behavior hurt you, she
continued to walk all over your feelings—with a set of stiletto heels. She
sounds like a shallow, opportunistic, solely self-interested person, who really only has room for one in her life: herself. Surely you deserve better.
And until you dump her and go find it, you're going to continue to feel
miserable. Tug your self-esteem out from under her Manolo Blahniks and
make your final exit without her.

THE PROBLEM OF SELECTIVE FORGETTING

I dated the king of jerks for a year. When I finally broke up
with him, I felt like I was starting a new life. But when I feel
a little down, I sometimes can't stop myself from calling him,
then we start up again. Why do I keep going back to a guy
who I know is bad for me?

Marnie, 33

Toronto, Canada

When people look back on their relationships, only the fond memories,
no matter how rare, come to mind. Nobody ever reminisces about how
their lover would pick an all-night fight when they have a plane to catch
early the next morning.

In a moment of loneliness, your ex-boyfriend's long list of faults—being jobless, miserly, a bully, not too great in bed, selfish, immature, and unschooled in rudimentary table manners (just to start)—pale by comparison to the attributes you suddenly value . . . such as the idea that he has a pulse and already knows your name and the buzzer number of your apartment.

If you are prone to going back to a bad relationship with your Über Jerk, try this protective measure to keep you from putting your hand back on the burner the next time you get a little depressed:

Sit down and fill a page with all of the things you dislike about him. If you find it comforting to elaborate, fill two. Document all the occasions on which he did unspeakable things to you that took weeks out of your life for recovery.

File your little deposition away in close proximity to your favorite antidepressants—your Prozac, your pot stash, Ben & Jerry's Chunky Monkey—or whatever substance you reach for when you get struck by the blues. Next time he starts to look appealing, take it out and force yourself to read the whole page aloud twice before you even go *near* a telephone.

REVENGE ON A JERK YOU'VE DATED

You suddenly make the unhappy discovery that your dream man or woman, who has on many occasions professed eternal, undying love for you, is really a lying, two-timing Jerk. You probably dream of telling the world just what a creep he is. Go right ahead. Draft a poster, make a couple hundred photocopies, and stick them up all over town at three A.M. with the assistance of your most adventurous sympathetic friends. Gil Karson, our tireless lawyer, just asks that we remind you to realize that this issue does skirt issues of legality, and asks us to state that we hereby abdicate all responsibility and sueability for any ensuing unpleasant results.

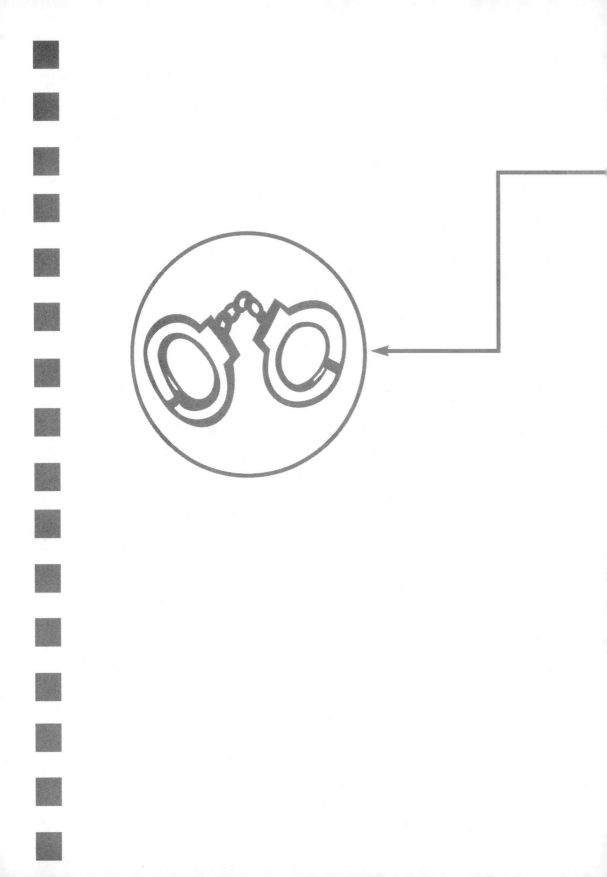

CHAPTER 7

The Relationship

How do you know if you're really in love?

People frequently drop by our Advice booth and ask us to help them decide whether or not they are in love. Unfortunately, unlike determining the need for electrolysis, the answer to this question isn't so obvious.

Is it love? Is it like? Is it lust?

Just as people feel compelled to put the eggs in the egg section and the butter in the butter compartment, they long to organize their love lives like they do their refrigerators. In fact, some people become so preoccupied with categorizing their relationship, then constantly checking to make sure it's living up to the definition they settled on, that they have little time left over to actually enjoy it.

Rather than worrying about what to *name* your feelings, instead why not step back and ask yourself, *Am I satisfied? Does my relationship make me content and happy—or not? Does the good outweigh the bad?*

People get a lot of their ideas about what love should be from the movies. If every moment of your love life doesn't feel like *Gone With the Wind,* it doesn't mean that you're not in love. Just remember that in Hollywood, they pay people to edit out all those scenes in which people discuss what can and cannot go down the garbage disposal. And heartache that resolves in ninety minutes is the sole property of fictional characters on-screen.

Make sure you've given your relationship a fair shot before you decide that you should move on. Unlike a Big Mac, love does not immediately reveal its full potential. A relationship must be nurtured over time before it can blossom into a real bond.

If you feel a continuing ambivalence about the relationship, explore whether your uncertainties might be part of a larger pattern. If you have difficulties making choices in other areas of your life, you will probably handle your love life in a similar way. And if you are skeptical by nature, you are likely to be skeptical about your relationship and perhaps harsh in your judgment of your lover.

To help clarify in your own mind how you feel about a person, you might try a little innocent comparison shopping. You don't have to run around and sleep with other people. But you might try casually dating a few other people for a little while to get some perspective on your relationship. Sometimes, a few weeks on the singles scene are all it takes to send a person racing back into the arms of the man or woman they "weren't sure about."

How do I get my boyfriend to make a commitment?

In a relationship, it seems like the moment that one person throws the idea of commitment on the table, the other hears the dull clank of leg irons being fastened.

In fact, due to complacency or stubbornness, or for fear of being alone, many people continue in relationships that have little vitality other than a virulent ongoing debate about commitment. Others, usually women stricken by overwhelming baby lust, are looking for someone—anyone— to fill the father-figure slot in their master plan.

Consumer culture seems to guide much of this panic to commit. Along the lines of the department-store "gift with purchase," many people assume that after putting a certain amount of time and energy into a relationship, they are entitled to endless unconditional love. Then they turn to the state for a written lifetime guarantee. It is unrealistic to think love will last just because you put it in writing and got it notarized by someone on the government payroll. It is one thing to agree not to have sex with people outside your relationship. But what if you or your partner change your minds about each other? Why would you want to try to force your lover to stick around when her heart has moved on?

If you have problems with your partner, if you love him and want to continue with him, try to resolve your problems. If many of your relationships seem to end prematurely, you should probably explore your romantic history for unhealthy patterns. But, in spite of whatever the world has to say about it, don't label yourself a failure just because a relationship didn't last. Anthropologist Margaret Mead had a wise take on this subject. When she revealed to an acquaintance that she had been married three times, he responded that he was sorry to hear about her "failed" relationships. She replied that they weren't "failures"; rather, when each marriage had naturally run its course, the partners went their separate ways.

Instead of creating a list of expectations for your future, try to accept the natural flow of your relationship. If you're happy and fulfilled, stick around. And when you know it's over, call it for what it is, and hit the highway.

Refusing to acknowledge that it's over could lead to costly dry cleaning bills.

PHOTO: JEAN MAHAUX

What do you do when the person you're in a relationship with wants something sexually that you feel uncomfortable doing?

One Saturday, on our street corner, a tall, good-looking guy parted the crowd in front of our table, and reluctantly sat down in our Advice chair. Blushing from head to toe, he told the pavement his problem. We listened in. His girlfriend was into bondage, he mumbled. He waved down the block at an attractive, well-dressed woman. "Is that her?" we asked. He smiled and nodded. The crowd behind him exploded with laughter.

He confessed that, while it was important to him to satisfy his girl-friend's desires, he was uncomfortable with the idea of participating in bondage. "I'm just a nice, normal southern guy!" he protested. He asked us if there was any way for him to get over his squeamishness.

In situations like this, people tend to assume the idea in question is all or nothing. He probably pictured himself starting his day in a rubber hood, a spiked necktie, and handcuffs. We suggested that he start small—with "Bondage-Lite": softer fabrics . . . velvet ropes, silken tassels. The fact that he was trying to meet his girlfriend's needs would mean a lot to her. And after his little venture into the unknown, he might even find it fun.

There are some limits, however. One of us, who will remain unnamed, politely declined the invitation to be diapered by a past boy-friend, on the grounds that there would probably be plenty of time in the future when diapers might be a necessity, not a matter of choice.

RELATIONSHIP ENNUI

Just months ago, the two of you were cavorting through a fountain in tuxedo and evening dress as the sun came up; now you're two inert lumps plastered to opposite ends of the couch, tented in matching I'M WITH STUPID T-shirts.

It's astonishing how quickly a torrid relationship can melt down into abject boredom. On average, the hot burning lust stage of a relationship lasts only about six months to a year. Keeping a relationship alive is hard work—practically a second career. If you love your partner and want to stay together, make an effort to reincarnate the electricity you both felt on your first few dates—and to rejuvenate the respect and kindness you felt toward your partner before you discovered the three hundredth tube of uncapped toothpaste. To recapture the early energy, pretend your lover is a stranger you're attracted to, and act accordingly. Start from the bottom. Men should throw out those gray, stretched-out briefs that have been cycling through the laundry since the early eighties. Women should wear sexy lingerie for no reason at all, and perhaps a reason will arise. Move up from lingerie improvement to renovation of other visual sore spots.

To combat the monotony of routine when an affair turns into a relationship, make an effort to add mystery, intrigue, and newness to your life.

Remember fun? Have a little, for a change. Inject adventure into your lives. Adventure is, of course, relative to one's particular circumstances. For some people, getting up from the couch would qualify as an adventure. For others, it could mean holding up the liquor store on Saturday night. Figure out where your limits lie, then go beyond them. Whatever the two of you think is two paces too weird or too wild to do . . . do *that*.

People often feel guilty about getting sexually bored with their partner. But it's human nature to be interested in that which is new and different. In fact, in very long term relationships, the sexual excitement often wanes to such a degree that, if presented with a choice of either having sex with your mate or mowing the lawn, you might seriously consider throwing yourself under the blades just to avoid getting between the sheets.

If you love your mate, and don't want to break up or cheat, you might try a few of the following ideas to revitalize your sexual relationship:

• Buy "how-to" sex books, read them together over wine and candlelight, and experiment with new stuff.

• Play Peeping Tom—at your own house. Take turns putting on "a show" and sneaking through your bushes to peep in at each other. Make sure your partner knows it's you, lest you spend the rest of your evening getting buggered in jail.

• Have a little cheap sex. If you're the man, buy yourself a purple suit at the Salvation Army. Buy your wife or girlfriend some trampy lingerie (new) and a big platinum wig. Make reservations at your local Motel Fantasyland, and messenger your love a note scheduling a clandestine meeting there. Bring a few candles to set the scene, and to complete the picture, wear dark glasses, act furtive, and sign the register "Mr. and Mrs. Smith."

• Try a little role-playing. Pretend to be the slave boy to the beautiful princess. Dress up in a dog collar and fulfill her every desire. Or you might play the role of the dirty old groundskeeper living in the toolshed in back of the big house who has a thing for the little rich girl.

Don't assume that you have to start wearing a rubber hood all of the time to keep your relationship exciting. Once you emerge from the bedroom, seek out outlandish new experiences. Don't be lazy in the planning stages. Just going out to dinner at a new restaurant isn't the answer. Instead, think of your life as a form of theater. Pick a theme and stage fun scenarios in exotic settings, complete with hairdo, makeup, and costume. Here are a few suggestions:

• Kidnap him. Pack his bags with appropriate attire, pick him up from the office, blindfold him, and drive him off to a romantic weekend in the country. If you have a lot of liquid cash or an unimpounded credit card, consider dragging him off to places foreign. Throw little love messages in his luggage, pasted together ransom-note style, spelling out just how much he means to you.

• Even cleaning the house can be sexy, if you do it naked, or in your lingerie. If you're a man, beware, when vacuuming, of experiencing the commonly reported incident of catching one's private parts in the hose of the Hoover.

• Have lunch in the middle of the nearest body of water. You'll probably be most comfortable if you rent a boat. Pack a lunch or buy one. Bring a breakfast-in-bed tray, some flowers, and a little music on tape. (Ten Thousand Strings do "Swanee River"?)

• Engage in sexy behavior in inappropriate places. (Tear off his pants in the parking lot.) However, unless putting on a show for Acme Security is part of the excitement, check first for video surveillance devices.

• Make an appearance wearing a disguise. Shop the costume stores, thrift shops, and uniform rental places.

• Get a set of erotic photographs taken by a boudoir photographer. Beware of making videos or taking photos yourself to save money, as it takes a professional film crew—as in director, cinematographer, *makeup artist*—to make people look good naked. Most people whom we know who have made their own erotic films tell us that they are almost unbearable to watch.

While the above scenarios can inject a lot of fun into your relationship, don't forget the romantic power of the old standbys:

• Buy your lover little presents. Let her know that she's always on your mind—even in the middle of a busy workday. The presents you buy don't have to cost a lot of money, but you may elicit a more enthusiastic response if you present her with an elegant trinket from Tiffany's than if you show up with a miniature mustache comb from the gumball machine.

• Surprise your love with a night in a fancy hotel near you. When you make your reservations, ask for a room with a Jacuzzi and other romantically suited amenities.

• On an ordinary evening, get home early and surprise your partner by cooking a special dinner. (If cooking is not your strongest suit, or if you are very busy, then *order* a special dinner.) Wear something sexy.

• When's the last time you bought him flowers for no reason at all?

• If you're giving your lover a present for a birthday, anniversary, or Valentine's Day, add a little surprise to the expected by setting her off on a little scavenger hunt to find it. Leave notes with clues that lead from one place to the next. You might even send her to a fancy restaurant to meet you, or to the airport to travel someplace exotic. Make sure you leave detailed instructions on appropriate attire, lest your mate show up on the beach in Hawaii wearing a ski mask. Also, use your answering machine as a fallback in case your written clues leave your lover stranded.

• Remember when you used to go out on dates? Continue to do so—preferably with each other. Schedule at least two dates a week, and stick to them. During the day, call the person in your life and say . . .

"Hi, this is Brian. . . . You know . . . the guy who sits across from you at the breakfast table. You know, lately I've been noticing how sexy you look, and I was wondering [act nervous here] . . . wondering if you'd go out on a date with me tonight."

Have a whole evening planned. Really try hard to impress her—just as if you were trying to woo her for the first time.

HOW TO WRITE A LOVE LETTER

Your mailbox is crammed with bills, bad news, jury duty requests, and unwieldy brown envelopes from Ed McMahon.

Think how you'd feel if you opened it one day and found a beribboned, scented linen envelope, addressed to "My Love." Inside the envelope, quill-penned prose sings your praises; your beauty, your warmth, your charm; how much you mean to your lover.

While almost everyone would like to *receive* a letter like this, most people find the idea of *writing* such a letter extremely daunting. Like Sunday drivers, it's been a little too long since they've gotten behind a pen to create anything other than a grocery list. Consequently, they feel completely inadequate for the task, and don't even begin to try.

However, even if you can barely spell; if your grammar would age a third-grade teacher; if you don't have much of a way with words; you should realize that almost any effort you make will be fondly regarded. In a love letter, what really matters is the inspiration you find in your lover, written with enthusiasm and heart.

When you write your letter, use special pen and ink and paper—remember, you're not corresponding with the gas company. And it's a good idea to avoid conflicts or unpleasant issues, or your letter may come off more like a request for couples therapy than a declaration of your love.

If staring at a blank page makes your knees weak, you might start by speaking your thoughts into a tape recorder. Just remember that writing your thoughts down is only the first step. After you've got a few words on a page, take your time editing them until you're happy with the results.

Here are a few more suggestions to ease the agony of the writing impaired:

- If you're no T. S. Eliot, instead of writing long paragraphs of prose, just make a list. For example, "100 Things I Love About You."

- If plagiarism doesn't trouble you, borrow a love letter from one of your friends, copy the good parts, personalize it for your lover, and sign your name on it.

- Get some beautiful handmade paper and attach souvenirs of your romance—photographs, matchbooks, ticket stubs—to commemorate the wonderful times you've spent together. Below each souvenir, write a little caption with something you love about your partner.

- Read her favorite poems on tape so you'll be with her even when you're not around.

- Copy a classic love poem in your handwriting (including credit to the original author), frame it in a beautiful frame, and sign it to him, from you.

- Even that rock you found on your vacation can be put to romantic use. Paint a simple love message on it and mail it to her at her office.

- Write down love-related quotes or lines from love songs on little pieces of paper from you to him, and slip them into the coffee jar, inside his dictionary, into his ratchet collection.

- When you're going to be away for an extended period of time, a friend of ours suggests you buy a stack of postcards, stamp them, and address them to your love. Every day put one in the mail with a short, thoughtful message. If you're really pressed for time, write all the messages ahead of time.

My wife caught me cheating on her and threw me out. She said she would never take me back, no matter what I do. Now that it's too late, I realize how much she meant to me.

Paul, 32
Boulder, CO

A woman can forgive many things, but catching her husband with another woman is rarely one of them.

If she'll talk to you, let her vent her rage. Don't try to justify or excuse your behavior. Admit you screwed up. When she's done smashing all of your bowling trophies, bend down on one knee and tenderly tell her how much she means to you. Then invite her to strap on a big dildo and teach you a lesson, once and for all. Afterward, tell her again how much you love her, that you miss her terribly, and you will do *anything* to have her back.

Realize it will probably take some time for her to start trusting you again. Be gently persistent. Let her know that you are sincere . . . that you realize the terrible error of your ways . . . that losing her is the worst thing that could happen to you.

It will not be easy, but you may be able to win her back over time. After all, she once loved you enough to marry you. If you can't win her back, you will have learned an important lesson of life: Decide which stones are diamonds before you go skipping rocks across the lake.

My boyfriend pressured me into telling him how many men I've slept with, and now he tortures me with it. (He's slept with maybe a third as many people.) Is he ever going to get over it?

Julie, 30
La Jolla, CA

It's a bad idea to tell any man the truth about this. A guy will plead, "Just tell me . . . it's important to me . . . I won't think less of you." In most cases, unless the answer is one (meaning him) . . . *Yes, he will.*

Many men still tend to have a double standard about sex. When they fling their seed around, they're "he-men." But, to them, a woman who's had more than a few men in her life is "promiscuous." They seem to forget fundamental mathematics. Although it takes two to have sex, somehow all of the women they've seduced shouldn't have slept with anyone else before them, and surely will never sleep with anyone else again.

In the meantime, build up his ego as much as possible. Make sure he knows that he's the best lover you've ever had—whether or not it's true. And if anyone else ever asks you this question again, keep the answer to yourself.

You're a woman who has just found your boyfriend in bed with another woman. What do you do?

Pretend you're Joan Crawford and do what they do in the movies. Drag her out of bed naked and shove her out the front door. Throw her clothing out the window after her.

You can either forgive him or get rid of him. If you want to stay together, try to determine what's missing in your relationship, then try to change things. If you really love each other, you may be able move beyond the incident.

You're a woman who has just found your boyfriend in bed with *another man*. What do you do?

See above. For a little variety, push the other man onto the fire escape and throw his clothing out the front door. Then call the police and report spotting a naked Peeping Tom holding a Presto-Log outside your window.

My boyfriend is extremely jealous. At first, I thought it was flattering, but now I'm tired of his accusations and verbal attacks. I feel like a prisoner when he demands to know where I am and who I'm with at every moment. Is there anything I can do?

> Hester, 34
> Detroit, MI

Unless you've given him some valid reason to believe that you're encouraging armies of men to rip your clothes off at every street corner, his behavior has little to do with you—and everything to do with his own insecurity. He may protest, "It's just that I care about you so much," but what this behavior really indicates is that he feels he is inadequate, and he fears it's just a matter of time before you figure it out.

Express to him that you need to be trusted, but don't expect miracles. There's very little possibility that a person like this will change—unless he has a burning desire to do so.

And because you're getting punished for imaginary sinful acts, you may eventually decide that you might as well make them realities.

I got dumped four years ago and I haven't been able to get over it. I still think of him frequently. Sometimes I call him and hang up. He is now married and has a child. I drive to their neighborhood and watch them sometimes. My friends say I'm mad.

> Diane, 34
> Roanoke, WV

You might as well be waiting for the Messiah to make a big entrance at the mall "food court." Sit down and face the facts:

> He dumped you.
> He married someone else.
> And he probably hasn't thought of you since.

To help yourself accept the cruel truth, give your relationship a formal, physical ending so you can get on with the rest of your life.

Have a funeral for your relationship. Collect all traces of your former love affair and bury them once and for all. For economy's sake, a shoe box in your backyard should do. Dress in black, buy flowers, light candles, perform last rites, and let yourself weep until dawn.

Then go back into the world and start your life anew. Remember the old French proverb, "Cure your broken heart in the arms of another." If all else fails, rent the movie *The Story of Adele H.,* to see how your life could end up if you don't let go.

ARE YOU OBSESSED?

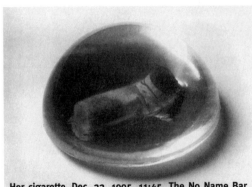

Her cigarette, Dec. 22, 1995, 11:45, The No Name Bar

- You move into his building.

- You get a job in his company.

- You marry into his family.

- You crack her answering-machine code and listen to all her messages.

- You steal his underwear and wear it to work.

- You build a secret altar to him and pray to it daily.

- You fetishize objects she has left behind, cast them in resin, and carry them around as talismans.

- You refuse to wash or shave the area where she kissed you on the cheek.

- If your obsession lives far away but visits your city on business, you frequently telephone all the hotels to find out if he's in town.

The Altar of Hope objects scavenged (clockwise from top center)
1. lock of his hair 2. his cross 3. rabbit's foot 4. his uneaten fortune cookie
5. love spell from local witch 6. items purloined from his trash 7. his half-
used bottle of Brut 8. his baseball hat 9. his crushed cigarette pack 10. his
half-eaten doughnut 11. a fork that touched his lips 12. his beard clippings
collected from the sink

"THE ONE-SIDED RELATIONSHIP"

by AMY

While living on the West Coast for a few years, I'd developed a viselike fixation on an L.A.-based doctor/university professor. Being in his presence made me want to donate my body to science. He seemed to like me too.

After several enormous hints from me, he finally asked me out. But numerous frustrating scheduling conflicts—births, deaths, funerals, mall openings—kept postponing our plans. At last, the night before I was to return to New York, we were to have our first date. All day, I eagerly anticipated the evening. I saw his face in my morning tea, heard his name in the whir of my juicer, and spent about eight hours putting together an outfit that looked as if I'd casually thrown it on at the last minute.

He was nearly an hour and a half late picking me up. Pacing my darkened kitchen, backlit by a huge, unsympathetic clock, I chewed what remained of my fingernails and wondered what could have become of him. The mocking shriek of the telephone jarred me out of my misery. With apologies, the doctor dispensed my bitter pill; moments after he'd finally gotten on the road, someone had paged him back to the hospital for overnight gunshot wound detail. The next morning, weighted down by self-pity, I flew back to New York, dragging my scraggly tail behind me.

During the next few months, I barraged him from New York with cards, letters, and the occasional humorous gift item. While he always seemed to enjoy hearing from me, he almost never *initiated* any contact. The Two Wise Women, Marlowe and Caroline, warned me to back off; slow down. Mulelike, deaf to all reason, I forged ahead.

Months later, when I was back in L.A. for a few weeks, after even further scheduling conflicts, we finally went out on our first date. After a romantic dinner, we kissed in the soft glow of the streetlights in front of his car. He asked if I wanted to drive up to see where he lived. I sputtered out my most nonchalant "Sure."

We motored up many dark and foggy canyon miles to his house, perched on the side of a steep summit. We sipped wine and kissed on the moonlit deck. When the night air grew chilly, we repaired to a couch inside, and basked in the warm glow of the fireplace. The fire began to make me a little drowsy . . . but his next words jarred me awake.

"It's two A.M.," he said. "I should drive you back to the hotel."

While attempting to sweep up the meager remains of my self-esteem, I tried to rationalize the apparent change in plans: *How nice,* I said to myself, *He doesn't want to sully our romance by sleeping with me on the first date.* We got in his car and retraced our long and winding path, my spirits sinking in tandem with our descent. When we arrived at my hotel, he asked me to go to the beach with him the next morning. Clutching a tiny flicker of optimism, I slithered blithely up to my room.

> Being in his presence made me want to donate my body to science. He seemed to like me too.

After a balmy day at the beach, as the sun was setting, he once again deposited me at my hotel. I politely invited him to join me for a nightcap. "Can't," he replied. "Tomorrow's a school day." Gritting my teeth, I flashed an understanding smile and rushed up to my room to examine my face in the mirror for signs of adult acne or impending leprosy.

We went out on two more dates; each one ending with him unceremoniously dumping me off in the hotel's cul de sac. Then, my very last night in L.A., he took me out for a seaside dinner in Malibu; crashing waves . . . romantic music . . . fine wine. I was staying at a friend's isolated cottage on the Venice canals. When we arrived back at the cottage, I threw my every remaining ounce of dignity to the wind:

"Want to come in?" I squeaked.

"I can't," he responded.

"But I'm all alone here and I'm scared," I pleaded.

He shook his head cheerfully. "Gotta be up early for work!"

Mustering an attempt at a smile, I thanked him for dinner and slunk inside, thrashing in tidal waves of humiliation.

In a one-sided relationship, the person you're interested in may make an occasional effort to communicate with you, but your phone calls or letters are usually not returned. You rationalize why he isn't calling you back: shyness, a hectic work schedule, long trips out of the country, sudden terminal illness. When you have plans with him, something "important" always forces him to cancel. He may take you out on dates, but only sporadically.

All the clues that he's not interested in you are jumping in front of you, waving and screaming, but you just turn your back, plug your ears, and go on your way. And in your imagination, the tiniest acorn of nicety becomes a giant oak of passionate love.

To temper wishful thinking with a dose of reality, have a "Moment of Truth." Like a detective at a crime scene, lay the facts out in front of you all at once, and objectively examine them.

Interview witnesses: all of the friends you've bored for many moons with the insignificant details of his behavior. You might even track down that stranger from the diner who listened to you the day your friends just couldn't take another word. What are their versions of reality, and how do they compare to your rosy picture?

Hopefully, evaluating the unfortunate evidence all at once will help you realize that the dead body on the parlor floor is yours.

"THE ROVING EYE"

by CAROLINE

When a certain type of male dons formal evening wear, he suddenly begins to feel very much like James Bond. His usual self differs considerably from James Bond, especially in the areas of height, weight, corrective lenses, and the ability to handle women and fast cars.

I entered a lavish party on the arm of such a man. He puffed himself up to his full height of five nine and a half, and made a prolonged show of delicately kissing the hostess on each cheek. He lingered at the hallway mirror, fluffing out his red silk bow tie and admiring his new waistline. We turned to work our way through the dense sea of velvet and creative black tie.

He paused to take stock of the crowd. I could feel his antennae unfurling like a snail inspecting new territory. As a well-toned Amazon brushed past us, he quivered with pleasure before quickly regaining his composure.

> I could feel antennae unfurling like a snail inspecting new territory.

We pressed on toward the hors d'oeuvre tray, held by a robust milkmaid type in French cocktail dress. I reached for a match, then turned to find him pretending to examine the pâté at close range, while peering intently down the milkmaid décolletage, like a professor of cellular biology at the microscope. Suddenly aware of my piercing glare, he abruptly stood up, his lapels and shirtfront now bearing an impressionistic imprint of the appetizer tray with a carrot curl that dangled jauntily from his eyeglasses, unbeknown to him.

When I returned from the bar, I found him perfectly positioned to gaze up women's dresses as they made their way down the precarious circular staircase. Engrossed in the admiration of two long model legs, he failed to see a round of melting brie that had just sailed loose from its tray and was now moving in a straight trajectory for his head. In seconds, James Bond was about to become Jerry Lewis.

My boyfriend likes to flirt with other women when we are out together. I've told him I don't like it. But he tells me I'm being too possessive. What should I do?

Natasha, 27
New York City

If your boyfriend is out with you, it's inconsiderate and disrespectful for him to be flirting with other women. Loyalty, sensitivity, and chivalry are the marks of a gentleman. The best way to reform him is by example. Let him get a taste of the action from your side of the table.

The next time you're in a situation where there are a lot of women he might flirt with, beat him to it. Take the initiative and point out some of their attractive features. Whisper loudly into his ear, "Can you believe that cleavage? It's out of this world! . . . And look at that butt! Wow!! What a knockout!"

If he likes to ogle women on the street, keep your eyes peeled and point them out to him first. If he doesn't get the message after a while, move on. Think of how unattractive this behavior will be when he hits seventy.

"LEGS"

by MARLOWE

At work, I was constantly fending off comments by a particular copywriter.

"Legs!" he'd shout. "Look at those gams!" Whereupon everyone in earshot would stick their heads out their doors and look.

No matter what I wore—a snowsuit would not have stopped him—he continued to amuse himself.

One day, I stepped into a packed elevator and noticed him standing in the corner. After casting a long look at him, I couldn't resist casually remarking, "Nice penis." All eyes immediately went to the previously described region.

Let's just say that, from that point on, my legs were no longer a topic of conversation in the hallways.

"LOST IN SPACE"

by CAROLINE

I was once in a relationship that was off and on so many times that I would need a calculator to tell how long we actually did go out.

We would be "on" for several months, then out of the blue, he would have a change of heart. First, it was maybe we were actually just friends. The next time, he needed a few months of "space."

Then, it was the wrong time of his life for a relationship. Then, there was too *much* passion.

Each time, I would drown my sorrow with a Spartan regimen of cigarettes, Milano cookies, and long telephone calls. Eventually, the angst would lift and I would resolve to be free of him once and for all.

My new freedom would begin with a trip to the bookstore for a soul-cleansing diversion, such as twelve volumes of *The History of the English-Speaking Peoples.* Once inside, however, I was drawn, as if by a magnet, to the bustling area titled "Human Relations."

There, I reveled in the dirty linens of love: the conversations between Mars and Venus, the women men don't love, Puer Aeternus, and even the criminal mind of the commitment-phobic. Whatever my latest problem was, I always found it, reenacted *Dragnet*-style with different names and the same gory details. My resolve would weaken further.

> . . . I would drown my sorrow with a Spartan regimen of cigarettes, Milano cookies, and long telephone calls

Unlike my cynical friends, the books said there is *hope.* If I could be more forgiving, empathetic, and really work on it, this failed relationship would once again soar.

And just as the books said, we always got back together, and after working through our conflicts, we would arrive at a plateau of tentative happiness.

After several happy months of being "on" again, we had just returned from a romantic ski holiday. He looked over at me from his pillow and said, "You know, I've been thinking . . ."

"Yes?" I asked in my best empathetic tone.

"I think I need some space right now."

Yes, a little space was exactly what he needed. About 150 million miles of it—whirling in a spiked, Sputnik satellite that would orbit perpetually through all the neighboring galaxies, teaching alien civilizations about the bachelor life form on twentieth century earth.

T minus six seconds . . . we have ignition . . . four, three, two . . .

THE OFF-AND-ON RELATIONSHIP

The Off-and-On Relationship begins the first time you decide to get back together on a "trial basis," continues when you have broken up and gotten back together over three times, and culminates when you don't know whether your RSVP for next week's dinner party should be for one person or two.

This emotional roller-coaster ride makes it hard to ever relax and enjoy your relationship, because you never know when the rug will be pulled out from under you. This state of anxiety spills over into the rest of your life: putting stress on the friends who have to listen to your problems, disrupting your work, and depleting the national supply of Kleenex and premium brands of ice cream.

You may already have tried to bring the relationship to resolution. But perhaps you are stubborn, willful, can't let go of the past; maybe you're even a bit of a masochist. One way or the other, you are probably out of touch with reality. We have created a simple assessment process to help you get a better handle on the facts. So, pretend you're an accountant, put on your visor, and add up what this relationship is costing you.

THE PAIN LEDGER

Now you've put this relationship in perspective. And remember that we haven't even attempted to put a price on hangovers, overused tear ducts, squashed egos, or lost opportunities to meet someone new.

If you're still crazy enough to want to salvage the relationship, then you need to find a way to break the on-again, off-again cycle. Stop using the exit ramp as a way to deal with problems. Dramatic exits look exciting in the movies, but in real life, the hero usually slams the door shut on his own foot.

Take the initiative in the relationship. Tell the other person how important the relationship is to you, and show that you are willing to commit yourself to it, instead of running away. Look at your problems together

The Pain Ledger

Telecommunications
- long distance telephone calls to share the grief. — $ 952
- access time to research problems on the Web. — 65
- Psychic Friends Network and 900-horoscope. — 439

Counseling
- therapy bills. — 3500
- co-dependency & positive thinking books. — 375
- church contributions, including costs of lighting candles before the Virgin. — 350

Travel
- Caribbean getaways to chill nerves. — 2,825
- costs of resoling shoes after too many walks in solitude. — 175
- Swiss sanitarium. — 4,500

Media
- purchase of depressing music about love. — 295
- rental of depressing movies about love. — 185
- books/magazines to divert attention from love. — 236

Food and Drink
- alcohol above normal bar inventory. — 1,278
- incremental chocolate truffles, potato chips, pies, cakes, ham hocks, etc. — 476
- cigarettes (resumed smoking). — 568

Worker Disability
- unproductive days at work. — 3765
- loss of job. — 10,600

Miscellaneous
- broken crockery, door hinge repair, stain removal due to tossed drinks. — 645
- detective retainer fees. — 2225

Grand Total — $33,454

and see if there isn't some way the two of you can meet halfway on the major issues.

If you are in a severe deficit situation, you probably already know what you need to do. Once you really let go, you will be available to meet someone who adds to the quality of your life, rather than driving you into Chapter 11.

WHEN NO ONE LIKES YOUR LOVER

"MURDER ON HIGHWAY ONE"

by MARLOWE

I can't say that I really disliked Amy's new long-distance boyfriend at first. I just found it a bit strange that he always hid behind a scraggly beard, sunglasses, and a brown suede floppy hat. The fact that he insisted upon wearing gloves to protect his sausagelike fingers from germs did not present a problem for me. Perhaps it was just that he refused to reveal his true identity for fear that if we knew just how "big" he was on the Hollywood scene, we would go into cardiac arrest.

> . . . he insisted upon wearing gloves to protect his sausage-like fingers from germs.

Anyway, I was in L.A. on a job with a female producer friend. We had just come from dinner in Malibu with Mr. X (he kept his gloves on to dine, and insisted the entire room was staring at him). We were driving along Pacific Coast Highway with our mysterious new friend in the backseat. There was an uneasy silence in the car. I glanced into the rearview mirror and found him half slumped over, wringing his hands and muttering to himself, "I hope I don't kill again tonight. . . ."

We let this comment pass and continued down the ocean highway until he ordered me to pull over so he could "relieve himself." Moaning, he slid out of the car, and vanished into the darkness. We waited . . . and waited. He seemed to be gone for quite a long time.

"Honk the horn," my friend urged, which I did repeatedly, until he finally reappeared, floppy hat askew, and limped toward the car. In the glow of the headlights, I noticed that the front of his pants was completely soaked. How disgusting, I thought. I guess it's hard to unzip one's fly with those gloves on.

... "I hope I don't kill again tonight ..."

Filled with rage, he crawled into the backseat, screaming that I had tried to kill him. Apparently, I had pulled over a little too close to the edge of the embankment, and his first step into the darkness sent him sliding down a thirty-foot hill of ice plants toward a violently crashing surf. He somehow managed to crawl back up to safety, narrowly surviving what he considered to be my premeditated attempt on his life.

I wish I had thought of this, I said to myself, as we pulled back onto the highway. Years later, Amy also regretted that I hadn't finished the job.

Your friends think your new love is pond scum in the swamp of life, and they're just dying to let you know.

First they drop polite hints. They ask you if you're really "sure" about your new lover. They tell you "you could do better." Then you start to receive party invitations that specify that you come alone, please. Perhaps the host will invite both of you but caution that everyone at the party will find your lover a bit "rough around the edges," so you might as well leave the person at home. And finally, the invitations just stop coming.

Decide what's motivating all the disapproval. Some people might dislike your lover because your taste is not their taste. Others will always step forward to be negative about whatever you are proud of. The very day you show off your newly shaven head, such people will snidely inform you that they've heard that floor-length hair is "the next thing."

If friends and family constantly try to force their opinions on you, remind yourself that your lover is not a cow you have entered in a 4-H contest. If they could offer you a blue ribbon for his well-shaped ears, then their ideas might merit some consideration. But what's really important is what *you* think about your lover. How you feel.

If you're the type who asks everyone for their opinion on the person you're interested in, you're part of the problem. Don't require whoever asks you on a date to run a gauntlet of your friends, acquaintances, neighbors, and fellow bus passengers before you'll commit to dinner. That's not romance; it's trial by jury.

If you've already opened the floodgates, and the general public feels completely free to comment with abandon upon your lovers and your life, it's not too late to dam up the opinion polls. Just firmly and directly tell your friends and acquaintances that you no longer want them to volunteer their feelings about the people you date, or about any other areas of your life unless you specifically request their point of view. You should likewise avoid volunteering judgment on your friends' dates and lovers.

That's not to say that you should ignore everybody's perceptions. When you're submerged in a fog of love, lust, and striking good looks, sometimes a trusted friend is the only one who can help you see clearly. Just be extremely selective about whom you allow to comment; ask one or two very close friends whose opinions you respect; people who in the past have proven to have your best interests at heart.

When a true friend shakes you by the shoulders and tells you that, in spite of the pillowside promises, all evidence points to the likelihood that your new love has never held a job, doesn't intend to get one now, is very unlikely to ever hold one . . . you should at least cup an ear in that friend's direction.

When you're alone, consider whether or not your friend's comments are at all valid—and whether or not the "problem" really matters to you. Then go off and do whatever makes you happy. If you choose to stay with a lover that your friends despise, at very least you won't have to struggle to find romantic time alone with the object of your affections.

PLAYING AMATEUR DETECTIVE

The three of us share a long fascination with the shady Chandleresque underbelly of life. Amy and Caroline spent most of their preteen years submerged in a pile of Nancy Drew novels. Marlowe has always had a soft spot for any job that comes with a steel police desk and electronic surveillance tools. Thus, when one of the security guards at the advertising agency where the three of us worked informed us that he was about to earn his private detective's license, we immediately began to pressure him for "freelance" work, as *"Operativos Privados."* We pictured ourselves in Chanel suits, at elegant restaurants, sipping fine champagne while spying on sly double agents with little opera glasses. The reality, of course, is cold cars, cold doughnuts, and even colder coffee, on all-night adultery surveillance in Queens.

While we never did get any jobs from our friend the guard, our passion for intelligence work often comes in handy when we try to size up people we meet—especially men that we're dating. Snooping is best done in the home environment of the person in question, where clues are usually abundant. The first rule of good detective work is maintaining a heightened awareness of your surroundings, including the commonplace details that most people take for granted. Don't assume that you have to dig through the drawers every time your host leaves the room. Just look around you with a discerning eye, and the evidence will present itself to you freely.

THE BOOKSHELF

Caroline was once disturbed to find *The Compleat History of Sex Crimes* tucked into the book collection of an otherwise mild-mannered man, who upon closer inspection began to resemble Richard Speck. Equally telling is the absence of a bookshelf or a bookshelf filled with something other than books, such as a large collection of Happy Meal figurines.

THE BULLETIN BOARD

Some people turn their bulletin boards into photographic trophy cases, displaying cheesy nude or seminude memories of their relationships, almost certainly not intended by the subject for postrelationship public consumption. Discovery of this kind of "visual scorecard" reveals a people-collector mentality in the owner.

THE MEDICINE CHEST

While this one may seem a little obvious, the careless may occasionally leave little medicinal treasures for you to happen onto, revealing weird ailments, contagious diseases, and bad genes.

COLLECTIONS

What does your date amass a lot of? Condoms? Wadded-up garbage? Hummel figurines? Lately, we've noticed a trend toward the collection of elaborate iconography of the self. One man plastered his apartment with gilt-framed congratulatory letters about his every accomplishment. A magazine writer one of our friends dated framed all of his rejection letters and hung them on his walls. Look for the flashing red lights, then make your own deductions about your date's personality and swollen or shrunken ego.

OBSESSIVE NEATNESS

- If all of the meticulously pressed clothes in the closet are hanging on matching wooden hangers, spaced precisely two and a half inches apart . . .

- If the floor looks so clean you could eat off of it, but you're afraid you'd sully the glow . . .

- If opening the medicine chest leads you to check behind you for photographers prepping to shoot the artfully arranged contents for a Clinique ad . . .

- If, every time you touch an object, your date runs over to properly replace it in its assigned position . . . like, if you take a piece of fruit from a fruit bowl and your annoyed date is compelled to immediately rebalance the bowl to the specifications of his fruit-arranging course . . .

. . . Chances are, you're in the lair of a compulsive neat freak, whose controlling personality is not likely to limit itself to the contents of cabinets.

TRASH BINS

Trash is usually a pretty good record of the last few days' activities: "Hmm, one marabou slipper, a crushed can of Colt 45 Malt Liquor, and a rotten artichoke." However, unless you're in the habit of accessorizing your outfit with latex hospital gloves, perhaps it's best to just peek, not poke.

MAGAZINE RACKS

Your date's magazine selections and weird catalog subscriptions will tell you a few things about his or her real predilections. So Mr. Professed Knee-Jerk Liberal subscribes to *Gun Country*?

RED HERRINGS

Be careful to watch for items that have been placed to whitewash or burnish the person's image in your eyes. One such oft-used prop is the very intellectual book lying on the bedroom night table. Your date is no more likely than you are to curl up in bed with Aristotle's *Poetics*. A diligent operative would examine the book for dust to discern how long it's been in position, unread.

A WORD OF CAUTION

If you get caught in the act, you are unlikely to be invited back to snoop again.

SNOOPING OUTSIDE THE HOME

People making inquiries among friends, co-workers, and acquaintances of the person in question are in grave danger of discovery. No matter how clandestinely you try to proceed with your investigation, word of your inquiries will usually travel—*fast*—right back to the one whom you were asking about.

If you feel you *must* investigate, be *very* discreet. And don't get caught.

One friend of ours, an L.A. lawyer-turned-screenwriter, received an unexpected phone call from the dean of the Yale Law School, informing our friend that someone had called to check on his credentials.

"Damn it," said our friend. "I don't want to work for another law firm."

"It wasn't a law firm," replied the dean. "It was a young lady."

I'm only interested in women that I don't have. Once I start dating a woman, I get bored with her and want to find someone new.

Gary, 30
New York

The problem is *you,* not the women. Once you have something, it's degraded in your eyes by the mere fact that you are its owner.

Step aside and build up your self-esteem before you encourage scores of women to develop an interest in voodoo dolls bearing a strong resemblance to you.

As your self-confidence grows, you will not need to prove your romantic prowess to such a degree. At about that time, your hair may begin to thin and you may be sporting "the tire look" around your abdomen. Suddenly, a long-term commitment may look very attractive.

I'm thirty-four and I'm not married yet. What's wrong with me?

Karina, 34
Manhattan

Nothing. It's just that, in any situation, it's always hardest to be the holdout. Every holiday, your parents sit you down and paint a picture of your dismal future in a cramped, dingy studio apartment for the rest of your days, with only a mangy cat for company. Yet, just because there are more of them (married people) than there are of you (single people) doesn't mean that they're normal and you're weird. They're all more concerned with you following their timetable and their pattern (so they can feel comfortable), than in you finding a person to share your life with who truly makes you happy.

Realize that a lot of people who rushed into a marriage at age twenty-five ran out almost as quickly to get divorced. Most people go through immense changes between twenty and twenty-five, twenty-five and thirty. Often, the companion a person is compatible with early on, isn't really right anymore after the person's personality and needs evolve a bit.

As long as you diligently maintain an effort to meet and get to know new people, you'll eventually meet someone worth spending more than just a few dates with.

My wife and I have been working really hard lately. It's been years since we took a romantic vacation. I have a chance to go to London on business for a long weekend, and I want her to come along. Problem is, we have two kids, three and four years old, and we've never left them with a baby-sitter before for more than an evening. Any suggestions?

Gil, 38
Manhattan

Perhaps you should try Child Time-Sharing. Think of a couple in your neighborhood who have kids close in age to yours; ideally, children that your kids really enjoy playing with. The weekend you want to go away, ask this couple to temporarily add your children to their menagerie. Promise to care for their kids for the same number of days that they watched over yours.

To sell this to your kids, positioning is everything. Try a Tom Sawyer approach. Tell them they get to go to camp for the weekend at the Zimmermans'. Make the whole thing sound like a lot of fun. When they ask what you're going to do that weekend, confess that you and Mommy would be much too sad and lonely without them in the house, so you have decided to go away and keep each other company until they come home from their weekend adventure.

My office mate says I scare men away by being too up front. But I want people to see the real me. If someone you're interested in doesn't like just plain old you, aren't they wrong for you anyway—and aren't you better off knowing that from the start?

Leslie, 24
Clearwater, FL

First of all, no one should see all of "the real you." Anyone who makes a practice of hair-combing or wearing deodorant will understand the flaw in this logic.

Romance is about mystery and intrigue.

Throughout your relationship, try to maintain the aura of being just out of reach. Realize that once someone feels they've "caught" you, essentially the game is over. Although, if you go this route, your relationship may take a little longer than you'd like to get started, but at least you'll be creating a strong foundation on which you can build over time.

Something worth having usually requires an outlay of effort. In love, that means setting and propping a stage, much as a playwright would, and consistently maintaining your audience's interest throughout all the acts. It's no small task. Consider this: After you've seen a play, have you ever left complaining that the play was too short? In a real-life relationship, creating and sustaining drama and interest is as or more difficult than in a work of fiction, and requires constant creative effort.

As you start getting to know someone new, don't be too eager or too available. In fact, throughout your relationship, you'll stay exciting to your partner if you can maintain a bit of this aura of being "just out of reach."

LOVE AND CAPITALISM

Dating follows the same principles as the market economy; whatever is available in large supply is usually accompanied by declining demand and a falling price. Decrease supply, and the price goes up again. In your dating life, strive to convey the image of a luxury product on back order, rather than that of the off-price outlet with large bins of irregular polyester panties on sale for two dollars a dozen.

I'm in love with a girl I've been friends with for two years, but she still just sees me as a pal. I've done a lot of nice things for her to try to win her over, but I don't seem to be getting anywhere. I'm beginning to feel this is a hopeless cause. How do you turn a friend into a lover?

> **Ryan, 25**
> **Scottsdale, AZ**

Even though you have yet to caress her tonsils, you probably know her better than any man she has dated. The bad news is, she probably takes you for granted.

Take some time off from your friendship with her. Don't be available every time she calls. This will elevate your desirability to her while opening new avenues in your social life—very important, in case her heart's impossible to thaw.

And no more Mr. Nice Guy. Treat her like you would treat any other friend. If she asks you to give her dog a flea bath, inform her that you've just run out of fleas. Be her friend, but don't be her doormat. If you want her to love you, you'll have to have her respect.

Now step in front of the mirror. Are you fat and misshapen? If she just wants to be your friend, maybe it's because she's not interested in seeing you with your clothes off. Transform your body so it's nude-friendly.

Then evaluate your packaging. Does your clothing tell the spotted tale of all you ate during the garment's tenure in your possession? Would even the Goodwill man sneer at the contents of your closet? If so, have a sister or a female friend with good taste to accompany you to The Mall.

After you've given her a vacation from you and you've done a little personal remodeling, touch base with her and see if your absence made her any fonder. Subtly drop the idea that you think the two of you could *never* be more than friends. It is human nature to want to contradict people. If you're lucky, your romance will begin with her telling you just how wrong you are.

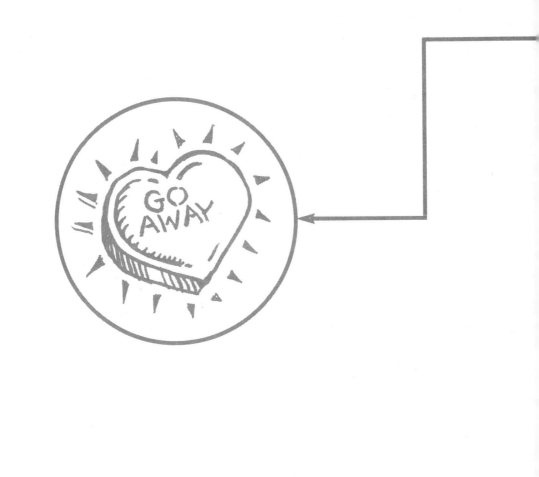

CHAPTER 8

Dumping Someone

"EVEN LOVE HAS A PRICE TAG"

by AMY

Valentine's Day was just too much for a certain boyfriend of mine to handle. A notorious cheapskate, he dumped me the day before— only to "decide" a week after all the cards, fine food, and flowers were due that he couldn't live without me. He seemed to have these strange emotional upheavals every time a present-giving holiday rolled around.

GETTING DUMPED

We never cease to be amazed at the novel ways people devise to exit a relationship. Your boyfriend suddenly decides to move but forgets to tell you where he went. Your girlfriend breaks the bad news by phone, via Federal Express, or the fax machine at your office. Or maybe you hear it through a third party—a friend, a neighbor, a stranger, the postman. We even saw a bit in the newspaper about a man who hired a skywriter to do his dirty work.

Why? Perhaps she loves you too much and fears being dumped herself. Maybe you were too much of a friend or not enough of a friend, or maybe his parents liked you too much or not enough. All you know is that just when you were getting used to the idea of being a "we," you are abruptly informed that you've become a "you" once again.

I just got dumped. What are some tips for recovery?
Lucy, 22
Brooklyn

If you're ending a substantial relationship, don't force yourself to jump right back into the mainstream. Allow yourself time to feel sad, even to wallow in your memories. Then mourn your loss in the self-indulgent style that you find most appealing. Buy seven days' worth of massage and use it up in one day. Take yourself on a tropical vacation. Eat a lot, drink a lot, and see a lot of movies—just skip all of the romantic ones. Don't forget the incredible healing power that can be found in changing one's hair. Color your hair some wild shade and buy a patent-leather miniskirt to match. Get the tattoo you always wanted—even a wash-off one. If you distract yourself enough, eventually you'll wake up one morning and realize that his head was really too big for his body anyway.

How do I know if I should dump someone?

If you're wondering if you should dump someone, it's very likely you should. And if you answer two or more of the following questions affirmatively, you're probably ready to move on.

• Do you notice their flaws all of a sudden? Moles and imperfections that were there all along suddenly appear to be growing larger, while vital organs seem to be shrinking.

• Have you begun to spot pieces from his wardrobe on *The Rockford Files*?

• Do the sounds of your lovemaking now evoke visions of a ferret having rough sex with Arnold Ziffle?

• Do you ask your partner to blindfold you during sex just because you can't bear to look? Do you ask your lover to tie you to the bed to eliminate the option of a speedy getaway?

- Do you leave him alone at parties, hoping someone else will hit on him?

NOTE: If your partner has begun to think any of these things about you, you are about to be dumped. Jump before you get pushed.

How do I know if *I'm* about to be dumped?

- When you inquire about getting together, they list a weekend full of fun engagements (to which you are not invited), then suggest that you "have lunch—sometime next week."

- They complain that you passed out, then snored all night loud enough to drown out all the garbage trucks . . . again.

- They wake up early the next morning and begin vacuuming.

- You get the answering machine late Saturday night and early Sunday morning. The return phone call comes Sunday night.

- They keep dropping hints that various office scheduling conflicts and natural disasters are likely to interfere with vacation plans months ahead.

- Claiming to be tired, they end a date. Through the rear window of the cab, you notice that they are heading in the opposite direction of their home.

- It's mid-August, yet they suddenly develop a burning desire to retrieve the argyle ski sweater they left at your place in January.

HOW TO DUMP SOMEONE

Be kind.

Even irritating people have feelings.

Be expedient.

The sooner you inform her that she's not the girl for you, the sooner she'll get over you.

Select from one of the following options:
Honesty and Its Variations . . .
Where on the scale does your admirer fall?

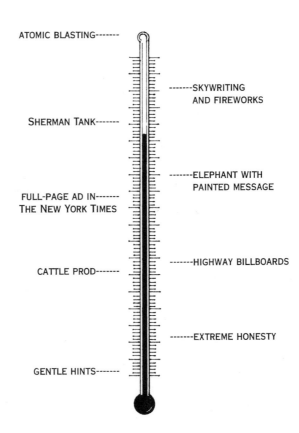

ATOMIC BLASTING-------

-------SKYWRITING
AND FIREWORKS

SHERMAN TANK-------

-------ELEPHANT WITH
PAINTED MESSAGE

FULL-PAGE AD IN-------
THE NEW YORK TIMES

-------HIGHWAY BILLBOARDS

CATTLE PROD-------

-------EXTREME HONESTY

GENTLE HINTS-------

"I just don't find you attractive."

Depending upon the strength of his affection for you and the fragility of his psyche, you could doom him to up to years of rabid insecurity and a lifetime Hair Club for Men membership.

"I just prefer thin women."
"I only date blondes and redheads."
"I couldn't have a long-term relationship with a bald man."
"I may be shallow—but you are worthless."

"There is another woman."

. . . And that person is always much more impressive in the jilted person's imagination than in reality.

"We just don't have chemistry."
"To me, you are seltzer water without the fizz—dirt unsuitable for planting."

"I just can't be monogamous."
"I'd like to have sex with just about anyone but you."

"I've really always been more interested in your best friend."

Not only are you dumping him, you're leaving him friendless at the same time.

"You can't afford me."
"Our backgrounds are just too different."
"I'm Park Avenue. You're Trailer Park."

"I don't think God wants us to be together."

"I'm looking for a religious experience and you are not it."

NICE THINGS TO SAY THAT DON'T WORK

While these excuses are not unkind, they tend to be temporary.

"I'm not ready for a relationship right now."

If you get involved with their best friend the following week, you will likely have earned a lifelong enemy.

"I don't want to have an affair with a married person."

Divorce is common.

"You're too old or too young for me."

Often leads to purchase and public display of unsightly rodentlike hair attachments . . . not to mention endless debate.

DISHONESTY IS BEAUTIFUL

When Keats wrote that the Grecian Urn said:

> *"Beauty is truth, truth beauty,—that is all*
> *Ye know on earth, and all ye need to know"*

he should have added a footnote that read something like:

> *"except when you are breaking up with someone."*

Many people are troubled by being dishonest about the reason they're ending a relationship. But a person with an overwhelming need to tell the real story in a breakup situation is more concerned with preserving her self-image as an upstanding champion of truth than she is with protecting the other person's feelings. In dumping someone, we advocate being a stickler for kindness over being a stickler for the truth. Do whatever you can to let your former mate leave with as much of his or her ego intact as possible. If you reveal the real reason you're breaking up—which might be something like "I'd throw myself over a cliff before I'd agree to sleep with you again"—you may do irreparable emotional damage to your soon-to-be former partner.

NICE THINGS TO SAY THAT DO WORK

Dull excuses usually work the best. They preserve tender feelings and self-esteem, helping you avoid dark voodoo curses on your body or your motor vehicle.

Here are some really boring examples which convey the idea that you were two equal partners in a good try that just isn't working out.

- "We're too different."

- "We've grown apart."

- "Our interests are too opposite."

- "We have different goals."

Such examples are a gentle way of conveying that, while you no longer have a grain of interest in the person, there's someone out there for everyone—even febrile, irritating, aspiring humans of his kind.

It may help to blame the breakup on the relationship between the two of you; not the person. For example:

- "I don't think we get along well enough to make it for the long term."

- "Because we spend so much time fighting, I don't think we have a long future together."

- "We want too many different things."

In other words, since the relationship doesn't seem to be working to your satisfaction, and is unlikely to last much longer anyway, you feel it's better to end it now.

If you've discussed big issues, like religion, where to live, and whether or not to have kids, and the person seems absolutely intractable on certain points, they may also be good excuses:

- "I don't want kids and that's not going to change."

- "I want kids and that's not going to change."

Just be careful not to use such excuses if you think that there's any possibility that the person will change his or her mind just to be with you.

NON-CONFRONTATIONAL DUMPING

Some people favor the unspoken approach to dumping someone; a roundabout, but often successful, method. The following are the two most frequently experienced examples:

Bratty Behavior:

You make an effort to consistently annoy or act cranky with the person you're dating, inspiring him to get rid of you, and thus preserving him from feeling rejected.

Dumping by Attrition:

You become less and less available to the person you've been dating until he or she either takes the hint or the relationship just fizzles out for lack of contact—usually around the point at which you can no longer evoke in your head a clear picture of the other person's face. (A little less humane than the above option.)

I've been rehearsing what I'm going to say for a week. Now I'm finally ready to break up with my girlfriend. The question is, where is the best place to do it?

Don, 30
Oak Park, IL

The best place to do it is in private: your house or her house—away from frying pans, knives, and other sharp objects, depending upon the volatility of your girlfriend. And make sure you have transportation alternatives available to you, because you're probably going to need them.

The worst places to break up are:

• Public places, especially restaurants.

- Somewhere distant that you've driven in one car. Someone will very likely be stranded or you'll be forced to drive back to town together.

- In bed, after having sex.

- While away on a weekend together—especially if you're with other people. Then all the world's a stage. You'll feel uncomfortable, your friends will feel uncomfortable. And the only thing worse than suffering in silence in front of a crowd is suffering loudly in front of one.

And don't break up by phone, fax, Federal Express, or carrier pigeon.

When Dumping Someone Isn't Punishment Enough

While riding up to her apartment in a crowded elevator, one woman friend of ours made an unpleasant discovery. From the back of the car, she overheard two women talking about some man, and realized that the man she'd been seeing seriously for nearly a year had been cheating on her the whole time with her next-door neighbor. Our friend wasted no time in telling this man that he and she were through. A few days later, she remembered that she'd left quite a few of her possessions at his place. As she still had keys to his apartment, she arranged with him that she would go retrieve her belongings while he was at the office. For moral support, her sister volunteered to accompany her. When the two of them entered his apartment, her sister, who lived near the markets in New York's Little Italy, removed a paper bag from her backpack and ceremoniously revealed its contents to our friend. Inside was a small hunk of Gorgonzola cheese. After our friend collected her possessions, her sister went to work. She cut the cheese up in little pieces, placed them in the base of his radiator, closed all the windows, and turned his heat up full blast. Although our friend was never able to get any accurate reading on the stench level in his apartment after the deed was done, about a year later, she heard from a mutual friend that the guy had been absolutely plagued with mice for about six months, and could never figure out why.

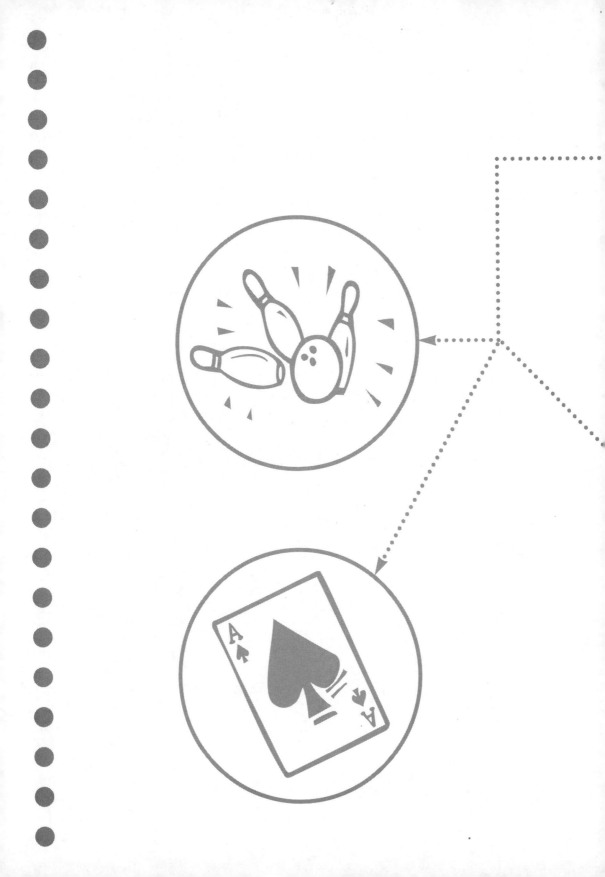

CHAPTER 9

Entertainment/Fun

Sometimes I go out with creeps because I don't want to be alone.

What's wrong with being alone? As long your brain cells still have a dial tone, you shouldn't be worried about boring yourself. We've come up with some suggestions for an entertaining evening at home that you'll thank yourself for the next day.

THINGS TO DO ALONE
(suicide alternatives)

DON A LEOPARD TUXEDO AND TRY YOUR HAND AT BARTENDING

Break out your Mr. Bartender recipe book and cover your coffee table with a kaleidoscopic array of fancy cocktails, crowned with creative garni that would make the tired paper parasol fold up in shame.

Start with the classics—Grasshoppers, Sidecars, Pink Ladies. Then concoct your own drink and ask for it by name in bars you frequent. Act astonished that they've never heard of "The Wobbly Cow,"—Yoo-hoo and vodka straight up.

HIRE YOURSELF AS AN INTERIOR DECORATOR

Put on a cape (a clean table cloth may suffice), and pretend to be an uppity French decorator. Tour your house, evaluating its entire contents—using the proper vocabulary, of course—"dreary, dreadful, despicable, drab, ghastly, godawful, hideous, unsightly, unspeakable, and wretched." Don't forget the invaluable "Where did we get *this*?!" (utilizing crooked index finger and a substantial measure of disdain).

Work up a redecoration plan. Then assess how many years and thousands of dollars it would take to transform your sow's ear. Then decide the best solution is to open another beer.

TAKE A TRIP THROUGH YOUR ADDRESS BOOK

Call people and hang up. Delight in the fact that you now know that they're still alive without the laborious effort of conversation.

GIVE YOURSELF A NIGHT OF
BEAUTY TREATMENTS

Try a glamorous new hairstyle, held together with kitchen utensils. Paint your face different colors with all your leftover beauty masks. Draw your blinds and try out daring makeup applications that have caught your eye in magazines. To test your new look, open the door when the Jehovah's Witnesses ring your bell, and see how fast their return visits subside.

PHOTO: BRITT CARPENTER

Why not try a French twist with a wire whisk?

VIDEOTAPE YOUR LIFE STORY

Should you nod out halfway through "The Story of You," change your tune. Tell the story of the person you'd like to be. Then compare the two of you and figure out what steps you should take to transform the life of Ratso Rizzo into the life of Mel Gibson.

TAKE YOUR DOG OUT FOR A ROMANTIC CANDLELIGHT DINNER AT A SIDEWALK CAFÉ

Dress in evening attire and give your dog a little bow tie so he won't feel left out.

TAKE A FASHION INVENTORY

Play mix-and-match with all your clothing. Take Polaroids of the outfits you create and tape them inside your closet door. Divide the outfits into categories: "Hire me. . . ." "Feed me. . . ." "Talk to me. . . ." "Have sex with me. . . ." and "Stay away from me."

GO ON A DATE WITH YOURSELF

Why stay home eating cold Kraft macaroni and cheese on Saturday night, just because you don't have a date? Make a reservation at a fancy restaurant and treat yourself to a fabulous meal. You might even buy yourself a rose. It's a good idea, however, to draw the line at kissing your own hand—pausing to exclaim, "Mmmm . . . I could learn to like you." Afterward, take yourself home and have your way with yourself in private.

DRESS YOUR DOG LIKE FAMOUS PEOPLE
AND TAKE PHOTOGRAPHS

PHOTO: ANDREW SHOTLAND

Buffy after breakfast at Tiffany's

A few suggestions: Benjamin Franklin, Gandhi, Marilyn Monroe, Andy Warhol, Madonna, Adolf Hitler, Bruce Weber, Abe Lincoln, Louise Nevelson, John Wayne, Elton John, Mother Teresa.

DO UP YOUR FAMILY TREE

Design a family crest using extinct animals and your family's favorite supermarket products. Create a family tag-line—like "The Anthonys. Buggery and Bad Credit since 1879."

CREATE A "HAVE DONE" LIST

Make a list of everyone you've slept with, in order of prowess. Include vital statistics. If you still have the energy, you can also prepare a "To Do" List.

TAKE YOUR FAVORITE DEAD AUTHOR OUT TO DINNER

It's been at least 146 years since anybody offered Edgar Allan Poe a good hot meal. Grab "The Pit and the Pendulum" and a few garments that Edgar might have been fond of and head out for dinner. Ask for a table for two. Toss Edgar's black cloak over his chair, and top it off with a matching stuffed crow.

Order a meal for yourself and another for Edgar. After dinner, notice out loud that poor Edgar didn't even touch his food: "And he hasn't even eaten for over 146 years." Ask your waiter to wrap it up, and pledge to rewarm for him later.

Wardrobe suggestions: If you're reading . . .
Carl Sandburg's Lincoln: Bring a top hat and novelty beard.
Krishnamurti: a clean white bed sheet will do . . . and so on

AD-ITUDE ADJUSTMENT

Tear out magazine ads you loathe and "improve" them. Marlowe once collaged a tribe of bedouins behind the proud gentry in a Ralph Lauren ad and nuzzled a family of wild pigs next to their prized dalmatians.

Once you've mastered hanging out with yourself, you're ready to hang out with the gang. Now you can enlighten the masses on how to have fun.

THINGS TO DO WITH OTHERS

"THE BAD PARTY"

by MARLOWE

It was my first date with my boyfriend, Ben. Around midnight, we stopped by a party he'd heard about, expecting to find it at its peak—you know . . . rhythmic pulsing, clinking glasses, loud chatter and laughter. Instead we approached an oddly silent door.

"Are you sure this is the right address?" I asked.

With barely one foot in the door, we were confronted by a suspicious hostess wearing one of those hideous, hand-painted cat T-shirts with sewn-on whiskers. She peered at us through large tortoiseshell glasses with upside-down temples, from beneath a tightly permed hair helmet. Her lips remained pursed as she scrutinized us with an attitude more befitting a desk sergeant at the Third Precinct.

After a thorough interrogation (Who are you? Who do you know here? Any recent convictions?) she took our jackets, surreptitiously patted them down for weapons, then hung them on a couple of bent nails a foot from the door.

We passed through a hallway that emptied into a large, intensely lit space. In the middle was a vacuous hole, the perimeter lined with party guests spaced like birds on a telephone wire. "Norwegian Wood" played on the portable hi-fi.

> "Norwegian Wood" played on the portable hi-fi.

The kitchen counter held the remains of what looked like a disappointing Thanksgiving; one enormous turkey carcass stripped clean as though by the most meticulous vultures, a bowl of ambrosia with soggy broken tortilla chips used in lieu of spoons, approximately nine beans remaining from a three-bean salad, a plate of sweaty cheese-cubes, the abstract smear of a melted ice cream cake on a paper doily, half a two-liter bottle of screw-top red wine, and one used plastic cup.

I spotted an anorexic scarecrow of advancing years alone in the corner, wearing suspenders and an undershirt of the shade that only occurs when the red socks are accidentally mixed in with the whites. He stood semimotionless, bent over, repeatedly bouncing a small rubber ball against the wall for a performing seal (the hostess's dachshund) to jump up and catch. When I politely asked the dog's name, the man froze in his hunched position. He allowed the ball to roll past him, turned, and slunk away, apparently not up for a discourse that involved complex conversation.

> For a brief three minutes it was one big hootenanny . . .

Well, okay . . . fine, I thought, looking for my date or something to attach myself to before actually having to talk to someone. I discovered Ben rolling his eyes over the few remaining tape selections. . . .

"Bread . . . Cat Stevens . . . Loggins and Messina . . . What's this? James Brown?"

"Put it ON!"

We started dancing, and the floor filled with other couples, most of them moving only from the hips down . . . arms hanging limp, they kicked their heels out to the side and up high behind them. For a brief three minutes it was one big hootenanny, until the hostess, perhaps frightened by the momentary episode of wild festivity, rushed over to the tape player and took us back to *Rubber Soul.*

After feigning interest in the hostess's dismal cocktail banter, we ventured to the other corner of the loft and came upon the "Zen Vow of Silence Ashram"—an alcove of ten conversationally strangled people sitting on the floor, staring at a table full of sand candles.

We tried to toss out a few witty zingers, but they only sputtered and fell to the ground, never even reaching deaf ears.

Having exhausted every possibility for a good time, we opted to leave this happening "be-in" for a more stimulating environment (maybe after-hours at the hospital cafeteria).

WHAT WENT WRONG?

First of all, the lighting was bright enough for an appendix operation. Harsh top lighting is about as flattering as holding a flashlight under your chin. Before your party, we suggest you remove half of the light bulbs from your fixtures, so the unwitting can't ruin the atmosphere you've created. You could string tiny Christmas lights throughout your house. Burn candles. Anything to give the space moody, seductive ambience.

Welcome your guests at the door, but don't fingerprint and strip-search the ones you've never met before. If you feel you can get away with it, you may, however, make an attempt to frisk the cute ones. "Hands up, bend over. . . ."

PHOTO: JEAN MAHAUX

If they served cocktails on the subway, rush hour might become "happy hour."

It's a party. Greeting your guests in an old sweatshirt may lead them to believe that they've just interrupted you while you were cleaning the kitty box. Wear something comfortable that puts you in a festive mood.

Music is, quite literally, the pulse of the party. If Cat Stevens is playing, don't expect the kids to be moshing in the pit. If you need a little musical direction, or if your collection is hopelessly dated, hire a DJ.

When you're planning the evening's music, remember that a successful party often extends beyond your expected time frame. It's good to keep at least one record on hand that could quickly evacuate Grand Central; any Neil Diamond, Glen Campbell, or for extreme campers . . . the seventies hit "The Great Elusive Butterfly of Love."

In case of a shortage of conversation, food gives your guests a way to occupy themselves. Unless it's a sit-down affair, it's wise to stick with food that's easy to handle. Watching your guests hover over a giant bird or rump roast, tearing its flesh free with their bare hands, is not a pretty sight. Party food should be sexy. It's more flirtatious to pop a tiny, tasty morsel into your mouth than to gnaw at a rubber bagel with dull incisors—another poor choice of hors d'oeuvres we experienced at a party. Besides, breads and other heavy dough products make dancing—or even standing—an extreme exertion.

Last, invite more guests than you need to fill the space. At a party, people welcome large crowds, as squeezing through tightly pressed groups of strangers is a way to meet each other and strike up conversation.

The following are some of our ideas for a memorable soirée:

ADVANCED PARTY THEMES

Unknown Artists Auction

(Ten to Twenty People)

Guests each bring a painting or sculpture—of the flea market/garage sale variety—that "speaks to them." Set the art up around the room, gallery style, while cocktails are being served. Guests can expound on the virtues of the dynamic tension and speculate what specific torment the artist seemed to be suffering from at the time. After a sufficient amount of alcohol is consumed, the guest who brought the painting presents and critiques it. Then the bidding starts (at a dollar, or perhaps twenty-five cents, depending upon the quality of the art). For five dollars you could walk out the proud owner of a fine oil portrait of Colonel Sanders.

From the collection of Stephen E. Clark

PHOTOS: ANDREW SHOTLAND

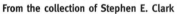

From the collection of Stephen E. Clark   From the collection of Stephen E. Clark

"My Left Feet" Night

(Ten to Twenty People)

With a group of friends, split the cost of hiring a dance instructor for a night of lessons. The person with the most floor space gets to be the host. Choose from ballroom, salsa, merengue, tango, hip-hop, samba, or western line dancing. Encourage your guests to dress to fit the theme. Be sure you provide enough to drink for people to overlook their lack of coordination. By the end of the year, you can all moonlight at Arthur Murray.

PROM NIGHT
(AS MANY GUESTS AS YOU CAN FIT)

If you were a wallflower in high school who never went to proms, this is your chance! Get a prom dress from the thrift store or a tattered powder-blue tuxedo. Decorate with the requisite thousand balloons and streamers. Borrow your neighbor's trellis, paste a big hand-painted prom sign on it, and photograph the memories. Invite everyone you know. Admission is proper prom attire, a bottle of champagne, and a corsage. After the festivities end, go to a diner in your tuxedos and frocks for coffee and pie. Fool around in the backseat to make it really true to life.

ANTI–FASHION-SHOW PARTY

(TWENTY TO THIRTY PEOPLE)

Everybody gets to (or is forced to) parade the runway. Ask your guests bring strange old clothing to contribute to a "grab bag." Throw in some kitchen or junk-drawer items to use as accessories—chopsticks, a turkey baster, a funnel, bubble wrap. Guests do each other's hair and makeup, with an eye toward reckless extravagance. Amid flashing cameras and applause, the group votes on the most stunning ensemble.

THE VALENTINE'S DAY MASSACRE

(AS MANY LONELY-HEARTS AS YOU HAVE ROOM FOR)

This is the gathering of the Valentine-Free. Dress is Amish Mourner. Celebrate your "independence" with others who sneer at little red hearts and chubby cupids with bows and arrows . . . just because they have no one to send them to. Black valentines make great invitations. As you seal the envelopes, substitute pink Maalox tablets for those annoying little Maalox-flavored hearts. Write unloving messages on them: "You Suck!" "Go Away." "Drop Dead."

MR. STUART'S HAIR EXTRAVAGANZAS

(TWENTY TO FORTY PEOPLE)

Our friend, Mr. Stuart, has been written up in *Vogue* for this one. A bespectacled research consultant by day, he is known to show up at dinner parties and whisk the women into the bathroom. One by one, they emerge in the most fabulous hairdos. The scene at the dinner table, lined with dozens of hopelessly chic, sexy women, gives late-arriving guests the impression that they've stumbled into a fashion shoot.

HUMAN SWAP MEET

(IT'S QUALITY, NOT QUANTITY, THAT REALLY MATTERS)

Throw a party and invite all of your friends of the same sex. The catch is, each invitee must bring an eligible, attractive, interesting friend of the opposite sex. Swear all of your cohosts to secrecy, or their guests may conclude that they're about to be auctioned off to the highest bidder.

FOOLS FEAST

(THIS ONE REQUIRES YOUR BEST FRIENDS AND ALL THE FOOD IN THE WORLD)

For the same price as dinner at a nice restaurant, you can have each friend contribute twenty-five to fifty dollars apiece and have the dinner of your lifetime. (You could even hire a chef.) Fill the evening with wine and ritual and lots of memories—sort of a *La Grande Bouffe* for your friends.

FOOLS FEAST II
THE "MEN ONLY" VERSION

(THIS ONE REQUIRES YOUR BEST *MALE* FRIENDS
AND ALL THE FOOD IN THE WORLD)

When this party is thrown for men only, it may end up resembling a Viking affair, with an abundance of meat, ale, and song. If you have money left over, provide animal skins for your guests to wear (acrylic toilet seat covers if funds are especially low). The general rule is to bring your own cutlery, or to go without. Videotape your ravenous friends as they tear into a venison roast with their finest dinner-sized Bowie knives. Sing and feast until dawn.

If you're a woman and you want to throw this version of the Feast for your female friends, invite everybody to dress in their best caveman drag, and outdo the boys detailed above.

STEPHEN CLARK'S FAMOUS
TUPPERWARE SOIRÉE

(TEN TO THIRTY PEOPLE)

Stephen's annual affair turns the Tupperware party into a real bash. He invites a mostly male guest list, all of whom arrive decked out as housewives in elaborate homemade aprons in hopes of winning first prize. Their favorite Tupperware lady comes each year, toting garbage bags full of plastic kitchen helpers, and displays a wallet full of photos of her elementary-school sons—at which the crowd coos approvingly, "Oooh, he's cute." During cocktails, she leads the group through games like Tupperware bingo, winners receiving weird plastic utensils that serve only one obscure purpose—like the spoon designed to remove that last stubborn olive from the jar. The guests pick up valuable kitchen hints and learn the lost art of lid burping.

Progressive Dinner

(Six to Eight People)

Eat your way from appetizer to dessert, all at different restaurants. "We'd like one Caesar salad, eight forks . . . and the check, please." If you intend to visit the restaurant again, perhaps you should invest in a little plastic surgery.

Wigstock

(Twenty to Thirty People)

As at New York's eponymous festival, all guests must wear wigs to get in. If your friends can't afford a trip to Bee's Hive of Hairpieces, suggest they make their own. This idea also comes in handy when you'd like to throw a dinner party but you are tired of the same old group of friends (chances are they're tired of you too). You'll have a moment's pause as you wonder how all of these strangers know exactly the same old dull stories your good friends always tell.

Dog's Day Afternoon

(Up to Fifteen Beasts and Their Humans)

Help your pet throw a party. Send paw-o-grams to all of his friends, who may bring their human companions if they wish. Bake doggie biscuits in the shape of bones and hand out party favors like squeaky rubber mice and rawhide breadsticks. Play music your guests will enjoy, such as "How Much Is That Doggie in the Window?" "Must Have Been the Dog in Me," and "It Must Be Puppy Love." Plan the seating arrangements with care, if you want the same number of guests to leave that entered.

ECONOMIC INSECURITY PARTY

(AS MANY PEOPLE AS YOU CAN AFFORD TO FEED)

This is a celebration exclusively for the unemployed. No one will have to answer the annoying question "And what do you do?" Refreshments will be modest, but everyone will feel free to stay late, even on a weeknight. Guests can share past employment horror stories and pass around the *Times* Classified section. It's sort of a twelve-step meeting for the job free—with cocktails.

BOTTOMS-UP PARTY

(FIFTEEN TO TWENTY PEOPLE)

If you've run out of party themes, and your life is otherwise empty, skim through the phone book and send out an invitation to anyone whose name even remotely comes close to *derrière*. Included would be "Bottoms," "Butts," "Heine," "Rump," et cetera. Dispense name tags at the door and encourage people to mingle. "Mr. Hiney, I'd like to introduce you to Mr. Rump." In case you're worried about the available supply of qualified invitees, here are just a few examples from the Manhattan White Pages: There are ten Butts, six Bottoms, four Rumps, two Arses, and many variations—including Bottums, But, Butko, Butz, Butto, Butensky, Butten, Heiney, Hino, and Rumph.

INVITATIONS

Create a party invitation that stands out from the crowd. Even the method of delivery can be unexpected.

A friend who once worked as a cook in Vermont told us of a time when he was checking in a load of chickens and noticed that the necks, livers, and gizzards were wrapped in wax paper printed with a photo of the proud chicken-farming family's new baby boy, Gus. We're not suggesting neatly wrapping your party invite around a fresh gizzard, but the same concept can apply to getting the message out to your guests.

"THE GOOD PARTY"

by MARLOWE

Recently, I attended a party given by several music industry executives in the East Village. The invitation specified that everyone bring an item an ex-lover had left behind, accompanied by a brief note explaining the circumstances. All of the items, some gift wrapped, were piled onto a table. Each guest took a number and when that number came up, the guest chose a gift to take home. The corresponding note was read aloud.

"Gifts" in the Pile Included . . .

- a pound jar of Kamasutra dust

- a wet/dry Dustbuster

- a pair of clogs

- two mangy teddy bears (one wearing heart-patterned boxer shorts)

- a skull necktie

- a skull ring

- a Christmas-tree stand

- a sexual trivia game ("tuxedo version," whatever that means)

- two hair nets

- a Felix the Cat Pez dispenser

- several books:

  Overcoming Sexual Addictions, Instant Defense Manual, The French Menu Reader, and *How to Get What You Really Want in Life*

- a military achievement medal given by a paratrooper boyfriend

- a cane

- two condoms with a love letter attached . . .

  . . . each paragraph beginning with *I want you* and ending with *I want you, I want you, I want you.*

Even at a party like this, people reveal their true selves. One woman, convinced that someone would snap up the wet-dry Dustbuster before her number came up, snatched it and hid it under her chair. When her number was called, the Dustbuster miraculously reappeared. She pulled it close and fled the room.

I came to the party with a butt-porno titled *Back Door Bonanza,* and left the lucky recipient of an ugly olive-green pen with an LED calendar readout, but traded it for a skimpy red teddy with a key to a hotel room in Kiamesha Lake, New York.

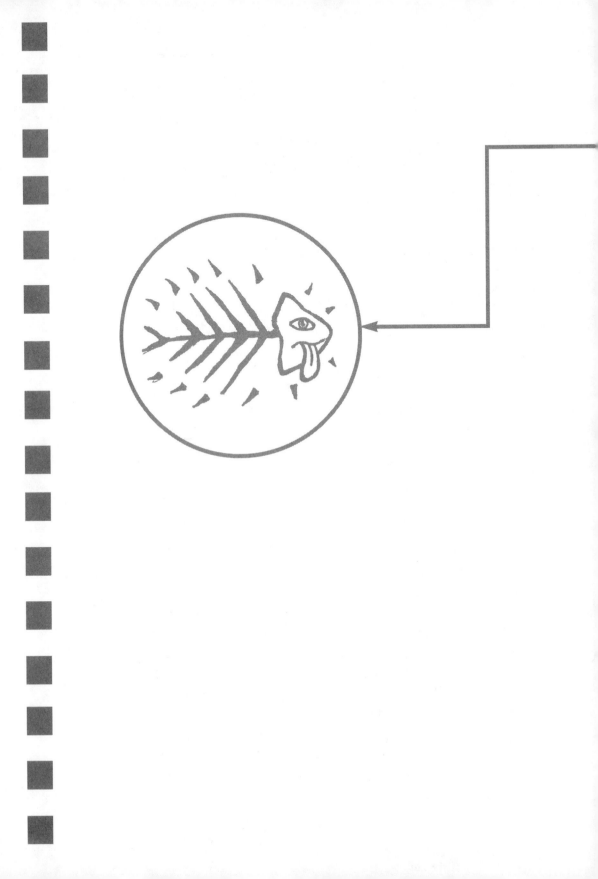

CHAPTER 10

Recessionary Lifestyles

*This chapter is devoted to showing you
how you can take the advice we've dispensed in the rest of
the book if you have little or no money.*

"AMUSING DINNER COMPANIONS"

by MARLOWE

It is a rare individual who has strolled down a New York City sidewalk strewn with tavern-tanned Bukowski types in soiled Chanel T-shirts and not thought, *Someday that could be me.*

For Amy and me, that day seemed perilously close, early one fall.

I was in the kind of relationship where, while confronting the bathroom mirror for a cathartic answer, I muttered, "I, too, can kill."

Rumor had it that the accommodations at women's prison were slightly less appealing than the high-priced West Village cell I was currently occupying, so the decision to extricate myself from this affair appeared to be the only sane thing to do.

Things weren't much better at my new art-director job at a particularly loathsome ad agency with a reputation of megamediocrity. I sold my soul in exchange for a fatter paycheck, until the urge to kill struck again. Before I could find the opportunity to follow through, only days after breaking up with my boyfriend, I was unceremoniously "let go"—in other words, fired.

Since debtors' prison went out in the 19th century, my worst fear was having no one to talk to all day. Those who had jobs knew instinctively to keep their distance, as though unemployment were a contagious disease that could somehow be transmitted through the holes of the phone receiver. I was destined to become a pariah, methodically wearing a trail in the carpet adjacent to my four walls, similar to the path a dog beats in the grass around the fence of his backyard.

> . . . as though unemployment were a contagious disease that could somehow be transmitted through the holes of the phone receiver.

My despondency lifted when Amy descended unexpectedly from L.A. in a similar situation—an unemployed renegade, fresh out of a parasite/host relationship. Together we schemed how to survive on a dollar a day without resorting to activities that could be deemed illegal by a less-than-empathetic jury of our peers.

Our primary source of nourishment became Happy Hour treats (wieners and fried birdy parts), and the consumable office-kitchen supplies of our working friends. We hailed buses instead of cabs, and when things got really bad, we even hitched a few rides on garbage trucks (sad but true). The day I extracted the very last piece of pink dry-cleaning tissue from a carefully pressed French cuff from my working past (toilet paper was a luxury we had given up weeks before), cold panic set in.

Hoping a little extravagance would lift our spirits, Amy and I decided to have brunch in SoHo. To conserve funds, we were

sharing an eggs Benedict (it divides easily), when Amy threw down
her fork. "This is ridiculous!" she declared. "We're witty, we're
charming . . . someone should be buying us lunch."

It was then we decided to use our advertising expertise in an
attempt to procure needed sustenance. With our last twenty dollars,

---

AMUSING DINNER COMPANIONS AVAILABLE
2 beautiful, interesting, creative women available
for dinner & witty conversation. You buy dinner, we
supply the rest.

---

we wrote an ad that we later placed in a downtown newspaper, *New
York Press.*

After "borrowing" a roll of toilet paper from the ladies' room, we
bounced home with lofty expectations. Surely, someone out there
was dying to watch two strange women eat dinner, and then pay for
it with his hard-earned money. That night, I drifted asleep counting
baby peas and other unborn vegetables that might someday grace
my salad plate once again.

At eight A.M., the day the papers hit the stands, we received our
first call. I signaled Amy to pick up the extension.
An overly caffeinated male voice nearly shouted
into the other end:

> . . . toilet paper was a luxury we had given up weeks before . . .

"Are you hungry?"

"Yeah," we chorused joyfully.

"Are you hungry for twelve inches?"

I explained to him that we were only interested
in the *digestive* organs. By noon, the phone began to ring off the
hook. It started to sound like the final hour of a PBS fund-raiser. We
proceeded to take "pledges" from stockbrokers, plumbers, policemen,
an inexplicable excess of computer programmers, as well as writers,
producers, and garment salesmen (one of whom held the coveted
patent to the elusive kurdemonium enzyme, allegedly destined to
revolutionize the garment industry).

An elderly woman called from New Jersey to reluctantly offer "a cheap Chinese lunch, but that's it." Even Meals on Wheels took pity on us. A guy with an accent as Bronx as Bugs Bunny said, "I feels sorry for youz goils—bo-diyez. I'll can be over dere in ten minutes wit' some samwiches." We demurred, despite cries of protest from our abdominal tracts.

Overnight, we had gone from a dearth of dinner offers to an overabundance. I put down *Berlin Alexanderplatz* in favor of the Zagat restaurant guide as my bedtime reading—crossing off the places we'd been, then adding up the stars at the end of the week like frequent-flyer miles. Our "companions"

> I put down *Berlin Alexanderplatz* in favor of the Zagat restaurant guide as my bedtime reading

seemed to feel they got their money's worth. After all, in between mouthfuls (sometimes during), they had the opportunity to speak endlessly about themselves, entirely absolved from guilt. (Therapists might consider the added value of incorporating the dining experience into their sessions.) During lengthy monologues, Amy would demonstrate her technique of rotating the plate and licking it clean, without the slightest interruption.

The best part of all this was completely unforeseen. Not only were we sating our palates with New York's finest fare, but we were being chauffeured in a shiny black Mercedes-Benz, complete with car phone, by our new servant, Kenneth, who had answered our ad with other thoughts in mind.

In addition to acting as our driver, this well-mannered gentleman was only too delighted to provide his services of cooking and cleaning; to act as our butler, masseur, manicurist, errand boy, and personal secretary. In return, all he asked was that we inflict upon him the most humiliating verbal discipline. We were to insist that he was utterly incompetent at his duties. The "firmer" our reprimands, the greater the pleasure we detected in his obedient replies of "Yes, madames, yes madames."

We were the envy of all of our female friends. Everyone wanted a Kenneth, who, on a typical day, would supply morning wake-up calls, complete with the temperature in Central Park, cappuccino deliveries, car service to job interviews (always with a copy of *The*

New York Times and a rose in the backseat), and plan business and social engagements. On one occasion, at a cocktail party, while maintaining the duty of keeping my wineglass full, Kenneth happily stood at his servile post in the corner, his name badge reading, HELLO, MY NAME IS . . . WORTHLESS.

The whole thing was truly a miracle. With a little creativity and three lines of type, virtually all our problems had been solved. In fact, our lives after the ad were significantly better than before disaster struck. However, there was one drawback. If the free meals kept coming at this rate, it would become necessary to make a slight amendment:

> . . . his name badge reading,
> HELLO, MY NAME IS . . . WORTHLESS

Two beautiful interesting FAT . . .

PROCURING FOOD AND DRINK

- Run your own "Amusing Dinner Companions" ad with a friend.

- Take your date to parties at which food will be served.

- If you'd like to invite a date over for a home-cooked meal and you don't have a lot of food, make it look intentional. Serve delicious Snack-E-Bobs! Say you have about half a piece each of ten different foods in your refrigerator (the last two olives, one baked potato, a heel of bread, one lima bean, et cetera)—put them all on a stick. Not only does it make eating fun, but to us, things always seem to taste better on a stick. You can even heat it over your gas stove if you enjoy that chemically flame-broiled after-taste. Apply grill marks with a small paintbrush and a little soy sauce.

PHOTO: ANDREW SHOTLAND

The happy couple, grilling

• When you're out on the prowl, free happy-hour wieners are no bargain if you're buying a lot of expensive cocktails. Carry a flask of alcohol with you when you go to a bar. At the bar, just order mixers—they're cheaper. Make a game of trying to fill your glass unnoticed. You might try distracting your drinking companion by pointing out aliens deplaning right outside the bar.

• Take a date to an art opening to obtain free glasses of bad wine and the occasional cheese nub.

• Throw a huge potluck dinner party at your house and invite your date over to help you get rid of the leftovers.

• When you're invited to someone else's house for dinner, or to a wedding, ask if you can bring a date.

• If you go out on a business dinner, order a huge porterhouse and bring the leftovers home to reincarnate and serve to your date as beef sukiyaki the next night.

• If you're going away for the weekend with someone, sing the merits of fasting and suggest you try it together.

INEXPENSIVE DATING IDEAS

• Pretend you're tourists and go see the local sights.

• Instead of dropping a lot of money in a bar, take a bottle of wine to the beach. Bring wineglasses and a picnic blanket. In lieu of nearby beaches, any nice grassy knoll with a view of the sunset will suffice.

• Spend the day with dead people! Tour the old graveyard together and take rubbings off the stones.

• Borrow a dog and take him out for a fun day in the park.

• Or borrow a child, and see how horrible it could be to have a child with your date.

• Bring the wilderness to you! Pitch a tent in your back-yard and roast wieners and some-mores. (Singing of "Kumbaya" should be avoided.) For authenticity's sake, no one should be permitted inside to use the bathroom.

• Buy your favorite play, read it aloud, and act out the parts.

• Go running, in-line skating, or biking together.

• Take your date to an antique show. If you'd actually like to add to your home furnishings, and you don't have any money, a promenade on trash day through a ritzy neighborhood often yields priceless exotic treasures for resale or personal use.

• If you live near a ferry crossing, take your date on a cheap cruise at sundown. If you have a little extra cash, hire the homeless to see you off and take pictures.

• Borrow a friend's penthouse and bring your date up for drinks on the terrace.

• Coffee dates: If alcohol is a must for you, carry an airline-size bottle of whiskey and make your coffees Irish.

• As people do with Chinese fortunes, go back and add the word *naked* to the end of each of these comments and do them again.

LOW-RENT ENTERTAINMENT

PARTY CRASHING

Properly dressed, projecting the attitude that you belong, you can worm your way into almost any event. Buffet weddings are especially tasty. If one of the bride's guests questions your presence, respond that you're a friend of the groom's, or vice versa. It is in bad taste, however, to leave bearing gifts.

Our friend Stuarto, a master party crasher, reveals an ingenious way to sneak into even the most seemingly impenetrable parties: Bring a standard-issue wineglass with you and pull it out just before you get to the door, to make yourself appear to be a person who's been in the party for hours and just had to walk out for a moment to get a little fresh air.

P.S. If all else fails, Stuarto recommends you go in the back way and sneak into the party through the kitchen. As a little added bonus, you may find an opportunity to take an advance sampling of a few of the hors d'oeuvres.

HOST SOMEONE ELSE'S PARTY

Offer to throw the party of a financially well-endowed, busy or lazy friend. Do all the work—from planning through execution, to arranging for *others* to arrive to clean up afterward. The only catch is, it's your friend's party, and he or she has to pay for it.

CHARITY CAN BE FUN!

Even if you don't have much money, you can still hang out with those who do. To break into the upper crust, when you read about a benefit someone is throwing, volunteer to be an usher in exchange for free attendance. Volunteer to work your local Emmy awards (through your local chapter of the National Academy of Television Arts and Sciences) to meet and hobnob with your favorite stars.

BUDGET MOVIEGOING

Tell your date you're playing a game called "Abduction." Blindfold him and ask him to get in the trunk of your car. Let him out after you pay admission for just one person at the drive-in.

ROMANTIC VACATIONS

Trade your apartment in the city for someone's house at the beach or in the country. To swap your tenement for a garret on the Left Bank, you might advertise in *The New York Review of Books* or other publications that feature a lot of house- and apartment-swapping ads. For really cheap flights, try courier services such as Now Voyager, 212-431-1616, and help chaperone a used liver to its new resting place.

CHEAP CHIC

Don't banish your faded shirts . . . your pants that have risen to flood-watch level . . . your jackets that have gone out of style . . . to the rag pile. With minimal effort, you can offer these forlorn garments a new life, while saving your limited funds for the purchase of much-needed bread and water.

WEARING YOUR DARK SIDE

The three of us are faithful followers of what we like to think of as The Cult of Black Clothing. While wearing black may simply appear to be a fashion statement, it actually affords many conveniences and opportunities not available to the more conventionally, more colorfully, garbed. For example, in head-to-toe black, you could pass for Amish, should the necessity arise. Your clothes never look dirty, no matter how seldom you pony up that pile of quarters at the Laundromat. And you're always ready to attend a funeral, should you happen upon an interesting one on your daily travels.

THE DYE VAT

When one of us gets a twenty-four-hour flu, or some other head-fogging ailment that leads to the unfortunate purchase of some cheery, colorful item, all is not lost. The Dye Vat is our favorite way to reincarnate our wardrobes. Most importantly, dying or redying your clothing black conceals the less than graceful aging of garments that seem to have been in your possession since the Johnson White House. If only face-lifts were so affordable and easy! When your redyed clothes start to once again reveal the march of time, just toss them back into the Dye Vat. Brand new!

Directions:

To make one pair of faded black jeans deep black again, throw three or four packages of dye into the washing machine, as per the directions inside or on the back of the package. If you are unsure of what color will evolve from your experiment, test the dye on an inner seam.

Note: 100-percent cotton takes dye best. Acrylic and other plastic fabrics don't absorb as much dye; your dye efforts may leave your garment industrial gray instead of black. For example, if you dye an ugly fluorescent green synthetic-fiber shirt black, it will come out a lovely mossy green.

After your dye adventure, run an empty washer cycle with a cup or two of bleach, or the next person to use the washer is likely to end up with a load of charcoal-gray underwear.

We never dreamed our faded clothing could be so black again!

PHOTO: BRITT CARPENTER

THE SCISSORS

Dull clothes, clothes that no longer fit, clothes that belong to old boyfriends, and other forlorn garments can be cut up, torn, frayed, fringed, or otherwise mutilated until they become new, more useful, more exciting pieces of clothing.

ADORNMENTS

Fabric trim has amazing restorative powers. We are especially fond of eye-catching kinetic trim, such as fringe and the rows of little balls often found lining the bottoms of drapes at eccentric aunts' houses.

INSTANT WARDROBE EXPANSION

• Borrow clothes from your boyfriend just before you break up with him. The danger of this approach is that it may prolong your breakup indefinitely—or until he gets his leather jacket back.

• Wear a beautiful and fascinating hat to draw attention away from shabby clothes.

• Offer to take care of people's homes, plants, and pets while they are away. (Only the homes of those who wear your dress size.) Wear their clothing to social events (at which you are not likely to consume red wine in the presence of clumsy people). Convince yourself that you are doing a good deed by protecting the garment from theft, in case your friends' house is burgled while while the item is on your back.

• Turn your pajamas into street wear. A flannel suit for the office. Belt it and tell everyone it's the coming trend. Wear a sexy nightgown as an evening dress. Accessorize it heavily, so no one will suspect its origin.

• The Swap Soirée: Gather nice clothes and small household items that just don't fit your body or your style. Invite all your girlfriends over for a night of trading. If your boyfriend annoys you, ask him over and exchange him for something that fits you a little better.

• Turn your toilet seat covers into fur coats.

• Recycle your surplus mink coats into toilet seat covers.

BUDGET BODY IMPROVEMENT

BUDGET PLASTIC SURGERY

If you need plastic surgery, but can't afford it, offer to trade something to pay for your medical costs. Type your way to a new nose!

PAID WORKOUTS

If you can't afford to join a gym until you get a job, combine your problems and go to work selling memberships at your local muscle palace.

BALDNESS

Why pay for costly hair transplants when the hair you need has been sleeping at the foot of your bed all along? Turn your pet into a toupee!

The Cat Toupee: A little dab of sculpting gel helps keep those telltale ears down all evening.

TURN SOCIAL EVENTS INTO INCOME

Dying to hold a big blowout, but you can't even pay the rent? With a concept that started on the West Coast (of course), you might be able to do both. It works something like this . . .

Say it's the twenty-fifth of the month. Your rent is $900 and you only have $750. If you want this to work, you can't be cheap. What you do is spend the whole $750 on the best party ever and charge $15 at the door. Advertise it in advance, leaflet the town, and hire security, a bartender, a band or DJ, and buy food and drinks. Properly budgeted, you should get at least a hundred people at $15 a head, which leaves enough left over to pay a cleanup crew—and hopefully, the landlord. It's not a task for the lazy, but with meticulous planning, it could be a fun way to deal with desperate times. Should you fail, your landlord will probably throw you out, and then your rent problem is solved anyway.

Even medical emergencies can be creatively financed with social events. Rely on friends and strangers to pay your way, without making them feel you're taking them for a ride. Our friend Mo Willems came up with a brilliant idea to pay for the repair of his chipped tooth.

He threw a party and, inspired by the success of large-scale rock benefits, named it "Tooth-Aid '93." For eight dollars, guests were entertained by live performers and served cocktails.

A good time was had by all, and Mo raised enough money to fix his tooth—and send it to Bermuda for a weekend.

Most magazines only TALK about health Care. ERSATZ does something about it with the presentation of:

"CHIPPY THE TOOTH," The Official Mascot of "TOOTH AID '93"

The Most Singular Account of the History of "TOOTH AID" in Words and Pictures.

1973: Mo falls off his bike. | He chips his tooth. | The nice dentist fixes it. | 1980: Ronald Reagan is elected. | Mo has a stormy adolescence. | 1992: Clinton is elected. | He promises universal health care.

New Years Eve 1992: Mo blows on a plastic horn. | He chips his tooth. | Mo has no health insurance. | Mo has no money. | Poor Mo. | Mo has an idea. | Tooth-Aid.

People like you support Mo & his tooth. | How? | By coming to Nada (163 Ludlow) | Saturday, Feb 6th at 10pm. | Give the person at the door $8. | Enjoy a full evening of entertainment. | What fun!

Your photo here. | Your photo here.

A PANORAMA project presented by ERSATZ, the magazine employing various parts of speech © Mo Willems 1993

Reservations Recommended

"POTLUCK FURNITURE"

by AMY

I kept promising to invite my friends over for dinner at my new apartment—"just as soon as I get some furniture." One day, while telling the same old tired story on the telephone, I looked around my apartment and took stock of my tables. I had café tables, coffee tables, dining tables, card tables, and even an oversized kitchen table that doubled as a desk.

All I really needed were . . . chairs.

The Chair Affair

You're invited to Dinner.

...but don't bring wine, little soaps, or pâté.

Just bring your own chair...

(preferably a solid, old wooden one that will fit into my Parisian Artist's Garret decor).

Paint it, adorn it, personalize it.

And carry it with you,

Saturday, October 20, at 7:30 P.M.

This idea can also be applied to improve other areas of your life that are lacking due to improper "financing." Are you short on underwear? Request that your guests "Bring a pair of panties! (Size six)" . . . and so on.

CORPORATE FUNDING

When you throw a party at your house, do as the big sports events do. Write to big companies asking them to sponsor your party. They'll provide free or reduced-price cases of product and huge, decorative banners you can hang across your garage: LAY'S POTATO CHIPS. BET YOU CAN'T EAT JUST ONE! Pick a beer, potato chip, and cigarette maker, and you may be able to throw a blowout free of charge.

TRANSPORTATION

- Invite attractive co-workers to car-pool with you.

- If you can't afford a convertible to attract the attention of people you'd like to meet, buy a used postal jeep for $800–$1,500, and turn it into a theme car with a funky repaint job. (Contact your local post office to find out when their auctions take place.) When you get bored with your Carmen Mirandamobile, buy a few cans of paint and glitter and transform it into Liberace's all-terrain limo.

FINANCING YOUR DATES

To combine meeting people with gainful employment, hang up a few signs:

RENT-A-HUSBAND!

If you don't have a husband of your own,
try the next best thing!

Are you going to the farmers' market, the flea market,
or Bergdorf Goodman? Your handsome "husband" will trail
adoringly behind you, lugging all of your packages
without a word of complaint.

20-year high school reunion fast approaching?
They'll all point and stare at your charming "mate."

Shopping for a new couch? A major appliance? A new car?
Bring your "husband" to keep all the high-pressure salesmen
away, then enjoy witty conversation over high tea.

Accomplished conversationalist.

Sympathetic listener.

Impeccable manners.

Versed in fine wines, opera.

Willing to cheerfully lift small
objects. Some light tool work.
Cannot saw.

Safe, dependable.

Solid references.

Best of all...
No annoying in-laws!

And I still have most of my hair!

WALTER STREJAN
555-1044

CALL TODAY FOR YOUR FREE ESTIMATE.

MORE MONEY-GENERATING IDEAS

- **Turn your chair into a piggy bank!**
Furnish your home with large, overstuffed furniture that releases your guests' pocket change when they sit down. Rate of change collection can be increased with skillful placement of unwanted paperback books under the front legs of the chair to enhance its incline.

- **Sell the side of your house as advertising space.** Skilled muralists will depict modern consumers enjoying fine American products.

- **Rent your lawn space as grazing area.**

- **Participate in cultural exchange while turning a profit.** Transform your front lawn into a youth hostel.

- **If you live near state fairgrounds, direct heavy traffic onto your front lawn with a flashlight and charge for parking.**

NOTE: Always keep your eyes on the pavement, in search of change and lost watches.

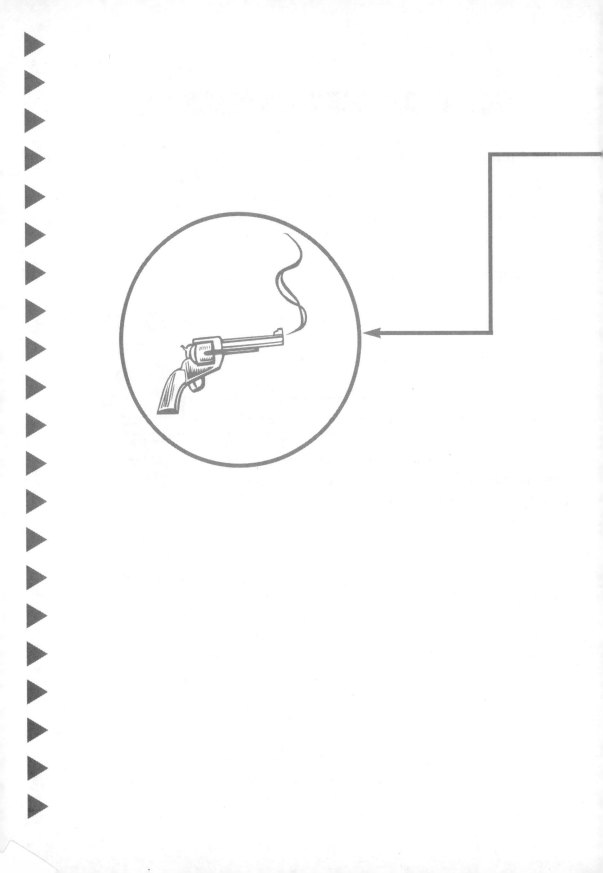

CHAPTER 11

Conflict Management

"MY LIFE AS A SINGLE HOUSEWIFE"

by CAROLINE

At a point when I was, as we euphemistically say in New York, "freelance," or "doing consulting work," I met a new guy. With a rather open schedule, I decided to do what every high-powered career woman fantasizes about. I would finally discover the pleasures of domestic life.

Dinner at my house with a boyfriend usually involved his procuring takeout while I reorganized my twelve-month plan and caught up on trade reading. Now, I would actually *cook* a meal.

Naturally, my new love was pleased with this domesticity kick. Unfortunately, it set a precedent from which it would later prove difficult to back down.

He soon viewed home-cooked dinners as his entitlement and began pushing for breakfast as well. Trying to avoid a conflict, I gave in on the breakfast issue. Then he wanted more variety in the menu. As it grew to resemble the Cordon Bleu syllabus, he began pressuring me to bake the desserts from scratch. Again, I failed to hold my ground and was soon at work weaving the lattice top on a cherry pie.

It seemed that each time I fulfilled one request, he was ready with five more. But I was so exhausted that I was losing my energy to fight back. I felt like I was looking out at the world from inside a cloud of flour.

Then he turned his attention to my shopping skills. He scrutinized the date on each milk carton. "Remember to reach way into the back of the case to get the freshest milk." He would have a fit if any product was even slightly marred. "This apple is missing its stem. Don't you think you should take it back to the store?"

> I felt like I was looking out at the world from inside a cloud of flour.

One morning found me bleary eyed at the stove, madly juggling the production of western omelettes, Canadian bacon, toast, fresh squeezed orange juice, and a pot of tea; trying to weave their diverging plot lines into the climax of breakfast. Meanwhile, he lay supine on the couch in his silk bathrobe, reading the *Times* and watching *Good Morning America.* Then he yelled out, "What the hell's going on in there?!! I'm hungry!! When's my breakfast going to be ready!!?"

I dumped the omelettes into the garbage can, pushed the toaster button to "Burn," handed him the spatula, and calmly replied, "How about never?"

NEGATIVITY LESSONS
learning to Say No

The average peace-loving individual may have very little acquaintance with the word *no.* It is considered, for the most part, distasteful, certainly not elegant, and almost un-American. In a "can-do" nation, reared on the promise of a better tomorrow, the person who says no is a quitter, a curmudgeon, and possibly even a Communist.

So, instead of saying no, the average person tries to adapt himself to a bad situation. Instead of being loved, he is "working on his relationship." Instead of getting paid for his skills, he takes on more work to prove he may be eligible for a two-percent raise in six months. Instead of having friendships he really enjoys, he is trapped on the telephone for two hours by someone who wants to "share" with him.

Let's compare his life to that of the person who doesn't mind saying no. The loud, ill-mannered beast who never hesitates to say no just got the corner office and the biggest raise of her life. She is presently relaxing in her luxurious penthouse apartment while her staff is working overtime on a crash project. Lying next to her is the man she recently pushed into marriage.

No is powerful because it shows people very clearly what you expect of your relationships. *No* demarcates the frontiers of your self-respect. Just as a dog will jump all over you until you give it a command, people will keep stepping on you until you draw the line.

It's time to brush those muddy footprints off your back and learn how to say, "No!" Not "I'm not sure about that, can I get back to you?" But "No! N-O! No!"

Start your "No!" training with a warmup exercise in your own home. Fling a window open, take a deep breath, and bellow, "No!" into the evening air—until your "No!" bounces off the distant mountain ranges and rouses the neighborhood dogs. Practice until you are satisfied that the pitch and resonance of your "No!" will stop a moose at fifty paces.

Now you're ready to practice with humans. Start by saying, "No!" to the mundane and the ridiculous and slowly work your way up to tougher issues. Here are a few exercises for beginners:

BEGINNER NO! TRAINING

• Get in the mood by watching old movies in which the hero takes the hard line. For example:

"Sweetheart, I won't play the sap for you. You killed a man and you're going up for it."

Humphrey Bogart
The Maltese Falcon

• When someone bids you a good day, say, "No, thank you."

- When someone asks you if you have the time, look at your watch, then reply, "Actually . . . no."

- When someone asks to bum a cigarette, take a long drag on your own, and answer, "Absolutely not."

- Practice negativity in your bathroom mirror every morning. Experiment with different facial expressions to get your point across, then add the word *"No!"* in a vocal tone to match.

ADVANCED NO! TRAINING

Say, "No!" . . .

- when someone you don't like demands your telephone number.

- to having sex when you are not really in the mood.

- to your hairdresser's bad idea.

- without giving any excuse.

- without feeling any guilt.

- And if someone looks like they want something from you, say no before the words can even form on their lips.

With rigorous daily practice of the No! exercises, you will eventually arrive at the satori-like state of transcendence over the problem of how to say no. One look at you, and people will stop even bothering to ask the question.

PROBLEM PREVENTION

Once you know how to say, "No!" you are ready to enhance your relationship skills in other ways.

Think about the aspects of your relationships that you may be sweeping under the rug—situations in which you've accepted compromise or even failure, because you didn't want to confront an issue. Perhaps you wanted to avoid a fight or feared the person might leave you altogether if you stirred things up too much.

Yet the reality is that whenever two people interact, there are bound to be conflicts of interest. Hiding from these conflicts doesn't make them go away. It just puts added strain on the relationship.

When you confront an issue, you stand up for what you believe in. You show the other person what matters to you. By taking the initiative, you can nip a developing problem at the roots—before it escalates into a major conflict and you're up against the wall screaming no.

PROBLEM PREVENTION EXERCISES

Look at the mundane situations in your daily life where you find yourself backing down from confrontation. For example, the next time someone tries to jump ahead of you at the supermarket checkout, speak up: "Excuse me, but I believe the end of the line is back *there,* not in front of me." Be firm and immovable, like a boulder. You will probably be surprised to find that most people will not only back down, but will also treat you with respect.

Proceed into deeper waters by scheduling some confrontations in your own life. Take a look at your relationships. If something smells rotten in Denmark, say so.

S A M P L E   C O N F R O N T A T I O N S

• If your girlfriend assumes that the two of you are in an "open relationship," address your differences before you get a surprise when you come home early from a business trip.

• If you found condoms in your boyfriend's travel kit when he came back from a business trip and you're wondering what's up, it's time to ask.

• If you found a pair of boxer shorts under your girlfriend's bed, and you only wear briefs, schedule a chat.

• If you are unhappy with your sex life, don't take refuge in the red light district; talk it over with your mate.

A word of warning: Once you confront an issue, be prepared to hear what you may not want to know. But at least you'll understand what went wrong and you can either fix it or move on to a better situation.

A S K   A N D   Y E   S H A L L   R E C E I V E

You are now ready to master more difficult challenges. It's time to start making requests of other people.

If you are not used to making demands, you might be inclined to say, This is not my nature and simply cannot be done . . . it's rather like trying to turn a hamster into a *Tyrannosaurus rex*. Not so. You don't have to be a hysterical maniac; just a grittier, more terrierlike version of your present self.

Asking for what you want will expose your ego to frequent rejection. Don't let this hold you back from action. You can go back to the well as often as you want. Each time you try again, you get another chance at achieving your goal, because people will see you more and more as someone who means business.

Begin the process by preparing a handy visual aid to help you construct your new image. Find a picture of a tenacious animal that you wouldn't want to meet in a dark alley—perhaps a puma, a Doberman pinscher, a hooded black cobra. Paste it on an index card and carry it in your wallet to remind you of your "inner puma" whenever you set forth to make requests.

Again, it's good to start small and work your way up. Begin with financial institutions and merchants, then proceed to personal relationships.

INTRODUCTORY REQUESTS

- Ask your credit card companies for lower interest and a bigger credit line.

- Renegotiate the payment plan on the big debt that's killing you.

- Refuse to pay for shoddy service or negotiate the price down.

ADVANCED REQUESTS

- Sit your lover down and tell that person what you expect from a relationship—if you want loyalty and commitment, demand it.

- Ask your lazy boyfriend to get a job today or get out.

- Propose to your lover—ask for a wedding.

WHEN TO DISCOVER YOUR NONCONFRONTATIONAL SELF

Having honed your conflict skills to a rapier point, you may feel tempted to meet every situation head-on like a snorting bull. Don't. There are times when running in the other direction is the wisest course. For example:

- a relationship that has entered the *Who's Afraid of Virginia Woolf?* stage.

- a boss whose executive role model is Stalin.

- an ex-girlfriend who is leaving dead rats in your mailbox on the nights of a full moon.

You might assume that you can solve dilemmas like these by reasoning with the person. But with these types, reason isn't part of the picture. When you try to fix the problem, you will be drawn into the vortex of fury in the mind of the maniac. If you escape, don't be surprised if you feel like

the comic-strip cat that barely gets out alive . . . with singed fur and a per-
manently crooked tail.

The best solution, in cases like these, is a speedy exit. Get out of the relationship, look for a new job, or contact the local authorities and let your
tax dollars go to work. Save your self-assertion skills for times when you
have at least a fifty-fifty chance of winning.

.....Where Do You Go from Here?

"THE RISE AND FALL OF A FRAGILE EGO"

by MARLOWE

It had been a frustrating morning, the subway ride pressed next to a particularly pungent type, numerous phone calls at work from people I detested, and the not unfamiliar chore of curing a hangover with Gatorade and tortilla chips. Fortunately, I had a shrink appointment at noon to air my disappointment with the world.

After the session, I was standing at an intersection making a mental list of the purchases I could have made at Barney's for the price of the consultation. A perfectly normal-looking man standing next to me interrupted my calculations.

"Excuse me, I hope I'm not being too forward, but I just have to ask you a question: Are you married?"

"Well, actually, no . . ." I responded.

"I can't believe it!" he exclaimed. "You're the most beautiful woman I've ever seen! Divorced? You must be divorced—"

I interrupted, "Well, I do have a boyfriend I'm—"

"He is the luckiest man in the world to have such a gorgeous woman. You tell him I said so—and have a beautiful day, pretty lady."

The light changed. I smiled politely and crossed the intersection.

I suppose I can consider that a compliment, I thought to myself, being one to whom street flattery does not cling. I kept smiling for a block or so until I was approached by a second man, also with a full set of teeth. Instead of the usual monosyllabic critique (legs, tits, butt . . .), I was the recipient of a compliment that, while lacking in grammar, at least contained proper syntax. "Girl, you got the finest set of legs on two feet. Mmmmm-mmmmm."

> He is the luckiest man in the world to have such a gorgeous woman.

What I normally would have felt as an invasion somehow seemed to be the appropriate comment a gentleman would make to a lady on the street.

My hair was blowing back. There was bounce in my step that hadn't existed a block ago. What's my problem? I asked myself. Things could be much worse. Evidently many people think I'm attractive; what am I seeing a shrink for anyway?

I lifted my chin a bit higher as I was about to pass the scrutiny of the patrons at the outdoor tables at a trendy café. Feeling as secure as I ever would that day, I spotted a man in a three-day beard and grime-flocked overcoat mumbling and shuffling in a path that seemed to be winding toward me. I maintained my confident stride.

At the very moment our shoulders were parallel, he clearly articulated one word:

"Ugly."

HOW TO LIVE WITH YOURSELF

Life is a lot like the streets of New York City. No matter what you are trying to do, there is always something double-parked between you and your pathway to Nirvana. In New York, it could be the person calling you ugly, or the dog poop clinging to your brand-new shoes.

In life, many problems begin with anxiety about what other people will think about you. This can cause a problem where none exists, or hold you back from some courageous course of action. If you take other people's judgments too seriously, you may ultimately find yourself on the path of least resistance: passive, complacent, and annoying to no one. A corpse with a heartbeat.

Don't be afraid of the person who calls you ugly, because coming around the next corner will be someone who is convinced that you should be the next Speaker of the House. You cannot predict, much less control, what other people will think of you. Your opinion is the one that really matters.

If you're bored or lonely or broke, don't just whine about it. Stand up and do something about it. Don't accept the status quo. Jettison the orthodoxy. Experiment. Push your life onto new horizons.

Your problems are the raw material of dreams and achievements to be realized. Every time you conquer a new problem, you'll see a slightly more interesting self staring at you from your mirror.

Get to know this fabulous person. Take your new self out on the town. Leave the old curmudgeon at home regrouting the bathroom tiles.

Don't be surprised if your new self starts dragging you out every night of the week in search of adventure. And when people see how much fun you two are having, they'll all want to join in on the fun.

Think of your life as a novel to be written. It's a set of blank pages with a beginning and an end. What goes in between is entirely up to you. You decide whether it's a mystery, a drama, a comedy, romance/adventure . . . a thriller! (One hopes you will choose to omit murder as an option.)

Do you have an intriguing plot? Or is the story going nowhere? Are the characters interesting? Remember that people really do judge a book by its cover. Does yours inspire people to open the book? Or is it simply too dull for words?

Every exciting thing that happens in a novel flows out of some other exciting thing that's already happened. So should be your life.

In the end, just get out there and take risks. You'll have more fun, you'll lead a fuller life, and maybe, if you're lucky, you'll even fall in love.

Before you venture out into the world, we offer you a few final words of advice . . .

- Always talk to strangers.
- Never have sex *before* the first date.
- Don't say "I do," when you mean "I don't."
- Never do as you're told.
- The party is never over.
- The worst things in life are free. The rest, get somebody else to pay for.
- Love means always having to say you're sorry.
- A dirty mind is a terrible thing to waste.
- Do others as you would have others do you.
- Don't knock loose morals until you've tried them.
- Do cry over spilt Veuve Cliquot.
- Early to bed and early to rise makes a man sexually frustrated.
- There are plenty of fish in the sea. Unfortunately, many of them have tentacles.
- You can catch more flies with a fly strip.
- Give him enough rope and maybe he'll tie you up.
- He who hesitates sleeps alone.
- You've made your bed, so have sex on top of the covers.
- Misery loves Prozac.
- The way to a man's heart is beneath his stomach.
- Blow your own horn if you can reach it.
- Never send in the clowns.
- Look, but leap anyway.

Best of Luck,
THE ADVICE LADIES